Learning to Cook in 1898

GREAT LAKES BOOKS

Learning to Cook in 1898
A Chicago Culinary Memoir

ELLEN F. STEINBERG

RECIPE ADAPTATIONS BY
ELEANOR HUDERA HANSON

Wayne State University Press • Detroit

11 10 09 08 07   5 4 3 2 1

Library of Congress Cataloging-in-Publication Data
Steinberg, Ellen FitzSimmons, 1948–
Learning to cook in 1898 : a Chicago culinary memoir / Ellen F. Steinberg ; recipe
adaptations by Eleanor Hudera Hanson.
p. cm.
Includes bibliographical references and index.
ISBN-13: 978-0-8143-3364-8 (pbk. : alk. paper)
ISBN-10: 0-8143-3364-8 (pbk. : alk. paper)
1. Cookery, German—History—19th century. 2. Cookery, Jewish—History—19th
century. 3. Cookery—Illinois—Chicago—History—19th century. 4. Frankenstein,
Irma Rosenthal, 1871–1966. 5. Chicago (Ill.)—Social life and customs. I. Hanson,
Eleanor Hudera. II. Title.
TX721.S73 2007
394.1'2094309034—dc22
2007013479

∞ The paper used in this publication meets the minimum requirements
of the American National Standard for Information Sciences—Permanence of Paper
for Printed Library Materials, ANSI Z39.48–1984.

Grateful acknowledgment is made to the Mary Dickey Masterton Fund
for financial assistance in the publication of this volume.

Pages from Irma Rosenthal Frankenstein's cookbook appear courtesy of
Chicago Jewish Archives, Spertus Institute of Jewish Studies.

Designed and typeset by Maya Rhodes
Composed in AdineKirnberg and Minion

To Jack and Ken
for their great patience
and understanding palates,
and, of course,
to
Irma

CONTENTS

Preface

This is more than simply a cookbook. Like most "instructional manuals for the culinary arts and repositories for traditional dishes," it does contain treasured family recipes and helpful hints, and, indeed, original recipes are given and then adjusted for modern cooks.[1] Yet, this book is not only a nostalgic collection of "receipts" from the late 1890s. It also follows and interprets the efforts that one young, middle-class Chicago bride, Irma Rosenthal, took to educate herself about cooking, nutrition, and economical household management. As such, it is a lens through which a certain period in American history can be scrutinized as well as a mirror reflecting contemporary knowledge and concerns. Moreover, it is documentation of rapid culture change, proof that "each generation imbued domesticity with its own set of cultural meanings."[2] Therefore, it is also an ethnography of cooking and cuisine in the classic ethnographic sense.

Cooking was never one of my consuming interests. Then I ran across an intriguing, crumbling pocket notebook. It had been tossed in with a box lot of diaries and memoirs written by the same person then stashed on the bottom shelf of a used bookstore's display case. On the cover of the booklet, a feminine hand had scrawled, "First Cook Book." Scribbled inside in soft lead pencil were recipes, most of which had been recorded in English, sprinkled here and there with a few phonetically spelled German words. Curious about the contents, and secretly hoping it also contained photographs of the author, I bought the box. Alas, there were no pictures of her as a young woman.

Once in my possession, I wondered if these receipts were simply utilitarian scraps of paper the author would consult while preparing meals. Or did they signify something else? Was there an internal logic to this collection? What information about the writer, her background, her social network, and her life could I tease out of the crispy brown pages of the small notebook and the associated diaries and memoirs?

Many of the handwritten recipes recorded on the cookbook's heavily toned sheets had rather obvious German roots. As it turned out, those had, indeed, been passed along around 1898 from an immigrant mother, Betty Rosenthal, to her American-born daughter, Irma—precious in their own right because of that but also scarce in the culinary world, since "immigrants traveled light. Recipes and knacks of preparation . . . sometimes were lost in specific families and communities because they had been lodged in the memories of the immigrants who did not successfully pass them down to later generations."[3]

The booklet also contained now-brittle clippings from late-nineteenth-century newspapers and women's magazines, which revealed the author's literate, English-speaking, middle-class status. Cupcakes and corn flour johnnycake testified to American influences, while a mention of soy meal and almond flour breads seemingly demonstrated an interest in new products and nutrition.

I never anticipated when I began perusing the contents of that notebook with its assorted recipe snippets stuck between the pages and the precious diaries and memoirs that they would propel me into the histories of the German community in Chicago, culinary arts, and the domestic science movement. The primary material in the recipe book covered approximately a single year in the author's life, from right before she married at age twenty-seven in 1898 until, as best as can be determined, a few months afterward. Coupled with statements taken from her later writings, this cookbook was a very personal record of her interests, thinking processes, and learning at that time.

Irma Rosenthal (1871–1966) was a Chicago-born Jewish woman of German descent. She was born on July 25, slightly less than three months before the start of the Great Chicago Fire on October 8, 1871. Irma's parents, Betty and Abraham, both from Germany, had met at a Jewish charity event in Chicago in 1868. They married six weeks later and began a family almost immediately. Like so many, Irma's relatives had been drawn to America by economic opportunities and promises of freedom. They eventually settled into a Chicago neighborhood where others shared their cultural *Weltanschauung* (worldview) and language.

In transplanted middle-class German families, both Gentile and Jewish, the women were the slowest to acculturate to American life. Their spheres of operation were typically their homes, their churches or synagogues, and their children. Unless economic situations forced them into the working world, they had no compelling reason to learn English. Most were literate, but they read German-language newspapers and books and wrote in that language.

Not so their American-born children. This urban, urbane, public school–educated generation was not totally grounded in Old World traditions. Like most young people even today, they eagerly sought out and embraced the new. What was new during the Progressive Era was reform, and it touched almost every aspect of life. Quite simply, progressivism shook up the established order in education, politics, business, industry, religion, and the home. And the home was the arena where the American domestic science movement concentrated its efforts. In terms of religion, many of the Jews of this time who claimed German heritage belonged to the Jewish reform movement, as Irma and her parents did. That movement, begun in Germany earlier in the nineteenth century and refined in America with the Pittsburgh Platform of 1885, altered much of Jewish life and religious practices.[4]

Irma's happy childhood was abruptly truncated when her father tragically died around 1877 from blood poisoning following a botched operation on an infected throat lesion. Thereafter, her mother and the five Rosenthal children (two boys and three girls) lived with Irma's maternal grandfather in the heart of Chicago's German enclave on the Near West Side. Acting as his housekeeper, Betty sewed, mended, cleaned, and cooked. The girls helped, as far as can be determined, with little else besides the dusting, a repetitive and mindless task Irma found particularly onerous.

Irma attended public high school in Chicago until she was sixteen, dropping out when she became anemic—she was simply too tired to concentrate. In her memoirs, composed mostly during the 1950s, she attributed her illness, the first of many such bouts with anemia, to tightly laced corsets (she was proud of her fashionable wasp waist) and to indigestible daily lunches for which she had substituted much more palatable sugary, glazed pastries. Soon after her recovery, though, she had to find a job. Casting around for a career, she settled on becoming a schoolteacher. After passing the "cadet" teacher examination, she began work in the Chicago public schools.

Irma reported that she loved her job, but it was simply not enough. She wanted, almost more than anything, to be a professional, published author. Toward that end, she assisted in the translation of the *Olat Tamid* (Einhorn prayer book) from German into English at the request of Rabbi Isaac S. Moses of the Reform Kehilath Anshe Ma'aiv (KAM) Congregation.[5] She also contributed to *The Sabbath Visitor,* a bright and entertaining periodical with a German section, and hired on as the Chicago correspondent for the St. Louis, Missouri, paper *The Jewish Voice.*[6]

Although she believed she had a natural talent for expressing herself, she wanted to learn how to write exceptionally well. She figured that to reach her desired level of expertise, she would have to take formal classes. Practically the minute that the University of Chicago opened in 1892, even before the first campus building was completed, she enrolled as a nondegree student— against her mother's wishes and somewhat in defiance of social expectations for young women of her social class.

Betty's fears that Irma would be branded a "blue stocking," remaining an "old maid" because she was a college student, seemed destined to become true. At age twenty-seven, Irma was still unmarried. Then she fell in love with her older brother's best friend, Victor S. Frankenstein, a Jewish medical student of German descent. They planned a November 1898 wedding. Irma, who up to that time had never so much as peeked inside a kitchen, suddenly realized she would be expected to cook for herself and her husband. With characteristic single-mindedness, she set out to learn the skills that were required. She solicited her mother's help first.

Irma bought herself a small pocket notebook—the inexpensive kind sold in school supply stores. The receipts and notes Irma jotted into that booklet while working in the kitchen with her mother learning the fundamentals of meal preparation clearly document how culture is often transmitted within the home. In addition, Irma clipped food-related materials from newspapers and women's magazines.[7] These were sometimes pasted onto a sheet but more often ended up simply tucked between two pages. These recipes show how extraordinarily adaptable American women were at that time and how fast traditional culture could, and did, change when exposed to new and pervasive influences and technological advances.

What Irma was doing in collecting those recipes and articles can be termed "cultural shopping."[8] First, she solicited traditional receipts from her mother and at least one of her mother's friends to provide a "base." Then, from among the many varieties of foods, newly introduced packaged products, and recipes brought to her attention in stores and through the print medium, she selected those she believed would expand her personal repertoire of menus and that would fit into what she already knew or wanted to learn about dietetics, hygiene, and household management. Finally, she folded the new into the old with interesting results—her "First Cook Book," a fascinating glimpse into the nineteenth century and cultural evolution.

ACKNOWLEDGMENTS

I am uncertain whether I can ever adequately express my gratitude to the following people whose advice and support were so freely given while I was writing this book: to Irma's grandsons, Ferd and John, whose supportive friendship has been a constant; to Mary Bordelon, who, after the first project, an edited volume of Irma's diaries and memoirs, was published, sent me back to my keyboard with the admonishment "The story's not finished yet"; to my good friend MJ Rinehart, whose enthusiasm for this project never flagged; to my mentor, Laura Bohannan, who, besides being a fine ethnographer, was also an excellent cook; to Eleanor Hanson, who has become a good friend and whose culinary expertise and willingness to experiment made the revised recipes suitable for modern cooks; and to my husband, Jack, for teaching me the most important mantra every researcher should know: "Let the data be your guide." I am further indebted to Joy Kingsolver, archivist, Chicago Jewish Archives, Spertus Institute of Jewish Studies, for permission to extrapolate material from Irma's cookbook, ephemera, and memoirs in this work. As always, any errors and omissions are my own.

$\mathcal{I}$NTRODUCTION

Irma began her cookbook in 1898 during the months preceding her marriage to an impecunious young medical doctor named Victor S. Frankenstein. She reflected in 1953:

> I soon found out [a] great truth about the art of cooking. If we were to eat meals, somebody had to cook them. . . . I elected myself cook and began the most useful activity of my career.
>
> . . . I resolved that if I had to cook, I'd try to be a good cook, and, furthermore if any one should be in the kitchen while I was cooking, that person would want to eat what I was preparing. I would never taste the soup or gravy . . . without washing off the spoon, taste it again for a further judgment, that if I had to wash vegetables I would wash them very clean, in other words, that the process, as well as the end result would be appetizing.[1]

Later, she attempted to put the recipes that she had amassed between 1898 and 1899 together for publication, with the following comment:

1

Men Like To Eat
And I Like Men
That's the reason I'm
    A Good Cook.
I shouldn't attempt to
    Write a cook book
If I weren't.[2]

On the reverse side of the booklet's cover, Irma copied a quote from George Eliot's *Romola,* a novel about a young woman who finds peace through faith and dedication: "Man can choose his duties as little as he can choose his parents.—Geo. Eliot."[3] My initial response when reading this statement was that it was an odd comment to place in a cookbook, and I wondered what it signified. I think Irma herself eventually explained in her later memoirs when she wrote:

> When, some years after [my marriage] . . . [Mamma] said that I was a better cook than she was and quoted a German saying that the pupil had surpassed the master [*Der Schüler hat über den Lehrer*], I felt an inner satisfaction, a recompense for the inner irritation that chafed because of the time consumed in the preparing and disposing of meals. But I always thought, in conducting of a home, that they were very important.
>
> Soon, however, I learnt the distinction between housekeeping and homemaking. Where housekeeping conflicted with homemaking I was fortunate to remember that Thoreau had said "To effect the quality of the day is the highest art."[4]

This book has been constructed around every one of the more than eighty recipes that made up Irma's "First Cook Book." Some came from women's magazines and probably from one or more of Chicago's daily newspapers. However, most of the handwritten receipts can definitely be classified as German, perhaps even as German Jewish. These were most likely learned from Irma's mother. Although none of these specified kosher meats or were identified as being "holiday" viands, similar recipes for sour fish, pot roast, grape pie, and green kern, green pea, and vegetable soups are to be found in Florence Kreisler Greenbaum's 1918 cookbook, *The International Jewish Cook Book: 1600 Recipes according to the Jewish Dietary Laws with the Rules for Kashering; The Favorite Recipes of America, Austria, Germany, Russia, France, Poland, Roumania, Etc., Etc.* The publisher's note at the beginning of Greenbaum's book identifies these receipts as "characteristically Jewish."

Irma made no annotations or marginal comments in her notebook, and nothing within its pages sets forth the logic underlying her inclusion of particular recipes or suggests why she had carefully clipped certain culinary and health-related columns. However, portions of Irma's own diaries and memoirs kept throughout her long life, though they were written years after her cookbook was initially assembled, do supply some explanations. Additionally, a close analysis of historical events, contemporary articles, and commercial cookbooks may also shed light on the rationale behind many of her selections. What emerges is a picture of a young woman determined to educate herself in the culinary arts and domestic sciences using whatever resources she could muster.

Chapter 1, "Preserving the Heritage," is a brief overview of the late-nineteenth-century German and German Jewish communities in Chicago and their shared culture. Chapter 2, "Leavened Bread and Cakes," contains Irma's recipes for cakes and breads and an explanation of the traditional importance of these foods in German and German-Jewish households. In chapter 3, "Traditions and Innovations," is an inventory of recipes Irma collected for entrées, sauces, soups, and accompaniments, as well as a discussion of them within the context of tradition and the burgeoning Chicago rail and fishing industries. Chapter 4, "Dainty Dishes," details supper and luncheon items, along with pastry recipes set into historical, socioeconomic contexts. Together, they reveal the breadth and scope of Irma's preparation for the future when she anticipated hosting elegant events for her friends and family. Chapter 5, "Of Cooking and Medicinal Foods," treats nutrition and dishes specially prepared for invalids, topics of singular concern to women as wives and mothers, who typically cared for the sick, but perhaps of particular interest to Irma because of her personal history and because her husband to be was a doctor. Also discussed is the effect that the domestic science movement had on literate, middle-class Americans, using Irma's saved newspaper and magazine recipes and columns as examples. The recipe section contains updated versions for all of the recipes mentioned in the book. It is my hope that those who wish can replicate these recipes with good results.

I have maintained Irma's spelling, punctuation, and sentence structure for the passages I quote as well as for the recipes she transcribed. She often used ampersands in her diaries and in her recipes; where I included diary entries, I substituted "and," but I left the recipes spelled and formatted precisely as Irma jotted them down. I inserted punctuation marks within brackets only where they might help the reader. German words have been translated in parentheses, with further explanations in the corresponding endnotes. For the materials Irma collected from newspapers and magazines, I have identified sources wherever possible.

Irma was, according to all who knew her, an excellent cook. She was also a witty and wise woman, full of German American *Geist.*

1

ℛRESERVING THE HERITAGE

During the 1890s "Guten appetit!" (Enjoy your meal!) was repeated at least thrice daily around groaning dining tables in Chicago's many German households. Intoxicating aromas of *Ochsenbrust* (beef brisket), *Apfelpfannkuchen* (apple pancakes), *Vollkornbrot* (whole-grain bread), and other comfort foods, treasured dishes for which women had carried the recipes from Old World to New in their memories and their practiced hands, continuously wafted out of open kitchen windows up and down the streets of the German enclaves.

The Germans had been drawn to this booming city on the shore of Lake Michigan in large numbers by grand prospects for commerce and industry, as well as by promises of freedom. Initially, they settled in Chicago's Near West Side neighborhood. As their numbers grew, they spread north, then farther west, and finally south, colonizing the open lands surrounding the city center. The 1893 *Book of the Fair* summarized their presence in Chicago: "There are at least 10,000,000 citizens of German parentage [in the United States], with more than 100,000 persons migrating each year from the Fatherland. And especially in Chicago does the German element make itself felt, the number of Teutons, either immigrants or of Teutonic parentage, far exceeding the Americans in number, and forming a most desirable factor in the composition of the body politic."[1]

More than one-third of the Germans in Chicago were skilled workers, lawyers, doctors, writers, and scientists. They quickly established their own businesses, social organizations, and houses of worship in self-segregated enclaves. Many, like Irma's grandfather, a bookbinder, were *Achtundvierzigers* (Forty-eighters), whom L. J. Rippley described as "usually well-educated and often in sympathy with liberal, even radically socialistic principles, who either fled or [were] expelled from Germany as a result of the unsuccessful German (and European) revolutions of 1848."[2] As A. B. Faust found, "In regard to the character of the German immigration of the nineteenth century . . . [t]here was on the whole a much larger percentage of men of culture in some of the immigrations of the nineteenth century. . . . The third immigration [wave] came after the period of 1866. They were mostly of the working class, with far better schooling than the same class of thirty years before."[3] Indeed, most of these Germans fit newsman George Ade's definition of the American middle class: "Theoretically, at least, there are no classes in Chicago. But the 'middle class' means all those persons who are respectably in the background, who work either hand or brain, who are neither poverty-stricken nor offensively rich, and who are not held down by the arbitrary laws governing that mysterious part of the community known as society."[4]

At least through the first generation, German was the sole language universally spoken, written, and read in the neighborhoods, establishments, and households wherever these immigrants settled, whether on the East Coast or in the Midwest. This was not new. In fact, as far back as the 1850s, an unnamed Danish traveler in the Milwaukee, Wisconsin, area had commented, "German houses, German inscriptions over the doors or on signs, and German faces everywhere. . . . Many Germans who live here learn no English and they seldom exit from their own German section of the city."[5] Had this writer walked through Chicago's German-inhabited streets during the 1890s, he would have made the same observation. Perhaps these conditions persisted because "Germany educated Germans felt themselves vastly superior to persons born elsewhere than on their orderly soil" and so felt no great pressure to change, as Irma once mused when reflecting upon early Chicago history.[6]

Yet, no American city's late-nineteenth-century German community was ever as cohesive or unsegmented as media portrayal and popular opinion would lead one to believe. Though unified by a common language, albeit with dialect differences, they were often divided along regional and class lines. This diversity of language and culture is more understandable since Germany was not unified as a nation until 1870."

These immigrants, along with their American-born children, included both Gentiles and Jews. Yet they referred to themselves simply as Germans. Recent scholarship on the German and German Jewish communities in Chicago reveals that "the German Jews were on friendly terms with the non-Jewish Germans of Chicago and identified quite closely with them. German Jews and non-Jews of Chicago spoke the same language, and in many instances they had been forced by common political views to leave Germany after the collapse of the revolutions of 1848. The German Jews read German newspapers, attended German theaters, and belonged to German organizations."[7] Most of the Jews, both German-born and of German descent, were solidly middle-class, urban, and urbane—similar to their Gentile neighbors. The external distinctions between them in terms of dress, speech, and work patterns were negligible. Even in terms of food, there were few differences.

By the 1880s more than 90 percent of the Jews in the United States belonged to Reform congregations. Reform Jews could make personal decisions about whether to keep kosher (*kashrut*) or not; many chose not to keep the older, traditional dietary laws.[8] Consequently, even food choices, culinary preparation, and meal presentations did not necessarily distinguish them from the non-Jewish majority. Perhaps this was one of the reasons behind the lack of overt anti-Semitism during that period. Carey McWilliams, however, believed there may have been another reason for the lack of anti-Semitism and conflict that later characterized some Gentile and Jewish relations: "[In] the period from 1840 to 1880, when the bulk of German Jews arrived, 10,189,429 immigrants entered the United States. Lost in this avalanche of peoples, the German Jews were numerically insignificant and aroused almost nothing in the way of popular antagonism or hostility."[9]

Unlike some ethnic groups who swarmed to Chicago during this period, the Germans tended to transplant their family groups, even if it took years to bring them over. With them arrived any number of Old World cultural traditions. Irma, during one of her many attempts to pen her autobiography, discussed her parents' families' immigration right after the Civil War:

Many Germans were emigrating to America. . . .

Papa came to America, leaving Germany alone, crossed the ocean on a slow going ship alone[,] landed in New York where Uncle Rudolph lived and practiced a trade he had learnt in Germany, that of being a baker. They must have been very poor. I recall hearing that Papa used to stand outside the bakery shop hungry, sniffing the good odors of bread baking and the cinnamony odor of coffee cake. Uncle J. the oldest of the 3 brothers who came to America, lived in Chicago. After a while came Papa and Uncle Rud. . . .

My two oldest [maternal] uncles crossed the Atlantic in sailing vessels about the time the Civil War ended (May 31, 1866). . . . Uncle Manuel, whom of course I never knew, was worried about his 7 sisters. What would become of 7 dowerless maidens in Germany, no matter how beautiful some of them were. In America women married who had no doweries—married rising young business men who needed wives. Uncle Manuel got a job and starved himself in N[ew] York to save to send passage money to some of his sisters and brothers left in Germany. . . . Uncle Joe came over, and Aunt

Molly and Aunt Kate, the oldest of the girls. . . . After her marriage in America, Aunt Molly, along with Aunt Kate and the 3 brothers who were in this country[,] managed to save enough money to bring the whole family to America, to Chicago where many of their neighbors had settled . . . [in] the little settlement of German Jews living around Fifth Av. between State and Van Buren sts.[10]

Early on, the urban blocks that the Germans colonized developed the *ordnung* (order), look, feel, characteristics, smells, and sounds of a *Kleindeutschland* (little Germany).[11] Speaking of those times, Irma had "a happy recollection of having gone to a German beer garden with trees along gravelled walks and of our parents giving us children big, fat pretzels and saying they wouldn't give us beer."[12] Others too have nostalgically recalled those same establishments as wonderful social meeting places, remembering that Sundays were a day when families liked to linger at German taverns.[13] These alehouses must have been fun places to frequent, as they would have been ringing with toe-tapping music and rocking with lively dancing and heart-stirring songs, all underscored by good (German) conversation, accompanied by enticing smells of rich, savory familiar food.

The larger city of Chicago must have been exciting too, with imposing buildings everywhere in the downtown area and myriad opportunities for amassing wealth, for social advancement, and for experiencing city culture. Yet, for most of the German middle-class women, life in the New World, as in the Old, revolved around *Kirche* (church), *Kinder* (children), and *Küche* (kitchen).[14] The same was supposed to be true for their female children, because, as Irma noted in her 1953 memoirs, "Girls were expected to get married and take care of their homes. . . . We were ladies—the original naming of the term lady was 'loaf-giver.' I interpreted that rather broadly as meaning [a lady was required] to embroider, play the piano, not use slang. I interpreted [John] Ruskin as meaning ladies must be useful. Later, after I was married, I learned to cook, because I felt that a loaf-giver should know how to be a loaf-maker."[15]

If food and its preparation provide perspectives on a society's values, then the pains that the immigrant *frauen* (women)
took in cooking and serving meals argued that Germans, despite
their religious diversity and localism, set a high value upon cuisine as well as on preserving their sense of *Deutschthum* (Ger-
manness). Their meals were kitchen tested, tasty, and nutritious:
fresh-baked bread or rolls accompanied by homemade jam and
sweet butter in the morning, a hot noontime dinner of rib-
sticking foods complete with dessert, then a light evening supper of cheese, bread, and cold cuts. Whenever visitors dropped
in, they were offered cakes and coffee, but the traditional time
for the *Kaffeeklatsch* (get-together) was in the midafternoon.

As Irma recalled,

> On Sundays our parents kept the roast goose or duck
> they were to have had for dinner at noon, for noon
> was the accustomed time for dinner, hoping that our
> father's friends, our mother's two unmarried brothers
> might drop in for a glass of beer or something good to
> eat. . . . [A]nybody who wanted could stay for Sunday
> night supper.
>
> As we grew up dinner parties were synonymous
> with holiday times and dinner parties after I was mar-
> ried and throughout my life have been in my blood.
>
> Several of our aunts lived very close by. They came
> in every afternoon to have coffee and *Kuchen* (coffee
> cake) with Grandpa after he had his early afternoon
> *Schlafchen* (nap). They reminisced, criticized, told each
> other about their children and husbands, [and] liter-
> ally brought their knitting.[16]

Although the women initially prepared traditional meals
from recipes most knew by heart in the Old World man-
ner, eventually certain American innovations and inventions
changed how they shopped for, fixed, and cooked food, as well
as altering what they bought. Just imagine—in Chicago, they
could purchase meats, poultry, fish, fresh produce from around

the world, and bakery goods all within a few blocks of their homes. They could line their pantry shelves with prepackaged, labor-saving commodities, such as baking powder, tinned peas, condensed soups, and bottled salad dressings.[17] They could cook their meals on gas stoves in modern kitchens that were not only lit by electricity but were equipped with both hot and cold running water and iceboxes. What a change even from the late 1880s, when, as Irma recollected, they only had gaslights for illumination and used burnt coal and wood in the kitchen stove.

Oh, those German women! Popular opinion did indeed set them on a pedestal. As late as 1909, Albert Bernhardt Faust expressed his unrestrained praise of the German American woman, whose virtues he felt were legend:

> Our country would not be what it is in vigor, population, and the bedrock civilization that comes from home training in her absence. . . . Historically, the emphasis laid upon the household arts, [such] as cooking, sewing, care of the house and children, by so large a formative element of the population from the earliest period of German immigration to the present time, cannot have resulted otherwise than in impressing the economic advantage of the principle and furnishing an example for imitation.[18]

They were seen by many not only as paragons but also as talented teachers of the next generation. Writing around 1899 in a letter to the *Exeter News* editor, Enoch P. Young asserted, "With such mothers [who were excellent cooks and homemakers], the daughters were sure to become adept workers in that line for the mother was ever looking forward to the future of her daughter's welfare and did what she could to prepare her, that she might go out into the world and fill with honor the part of wife and mother, the grandest and proudest position a woman can fill, queen of the home, the longest loved, the last forgotten."[19]

However, at least one contemporary author, M. E. K. Rundell, expressed concern that the generational passing of domestic knowledge was being neglected by some—that young women, both German and non-German, were no longer being instructed in household management or advised about how to be good wives and mothers. She offered a solution, a cookbook called *The Experienced American Housekeeper; or, Domestic Cookery Formed on Principles of Economy for the Use of Private Families* (1833) in which she first bemoaned the deplorable state of current affairs before setting out procedures to rectify the situation: "In the variety of female acquirements, though domestic occupations stand not so high in esteem as they formerly did, yet when neglected they produce such human misery. There was a time when ladies knew nothing beyond their own family concerns; but in the present day there are many who know nothing about them. Each of these extremes should be avoided; but is there no way to unite in the female character, cultivation of talents and habits of usefulness?"[20]

Then, in 1869 two sisters, both famous writers, Catharine Beecher and Harriet Beecher Stowe, collaborated in writing *American Woman's Home; or, Principles of Domestic Science,* probably to fill the same gap. A review of this work published in the *Manufacturer and Builder* magazine stated, "The range of subjects discussed is very wide, embracing furnishing, decoration, ventilation, heating, and general housekeeping . . . the care of personal health; nursing of the sick . . . wholesome food and drinks; home duties and amusements; hints on good cooking . . . in short, the whole round of domestic economy."[21] A later synopsis in the *New Englander and Yale Review* discussed the authors' contention that women "need special culture for home duties . . . women [need to be] thoroughly taught the principles of domestic economy, and trained with reference to their profession as 'house-keepers and health-keepers.' . . . Its hints on various departments of domestic economy, its suggestions about the necessities of body and mind, and its advice about the care of the aged, the sick, the ignorant . . . will prove salutary in thousands of families."[22]

Of course, German-language newspapers printed recipes, and there were cookbooks written in German that treated those same subjects. Beyond a doubt, the most popular was Henriette Davidis's *Praktisches Kochbuch für die Deutschen in Amerika* (Practical Cookbook for Germans in America).[23] This tome went through many American editions put out by various publishers, Georg Brumder and C. N. Caspar among them. The publishers' initial nod to American cooks was that measurements were no longer listed by weight but by volume. Each succeeding Caspar edition included more recipe titles written in English and incorporated larger numbers of ingredients specifically chosen for American kitchens, both of which reflected the increasing acculturation of its readers.[24]

Around midcentury, there was a movement to apply scientific principles and technological advances to the domestic sphere. Janet Theophano documents that "standardization of recipes occurred around the turn of the century with the birth of the domestic science movement. At this time, the modern format of a list of ingredients followed by directions began to be used."[25] Certainly, accomplished cooks knew "the sciences and art of cooking [are] divided into a few principle parts; the rest is all fancy. These parts are baking, boiling, broiling, frying, roasting, seasoning, simmering and stewing. Tasting is an adjunct to all."[26]

Irma realized, though, that it took a bit more than simply knowing the how-tos—whether gleaned from watching her mother or from reading in a book—to become a good cook. It took practice and attention to details, along with a solid knowledge of science, nutrition, hygiene, and health. And it took a willingness to learn from mistakes. Sometime during 1958, while bemoaning her many culinary disasters, Irma figured out that "I am a good cook *because* I have made so many mistakes." Continuing in that same vein, she also recalled that early on "[my] cousin Birdie reminded me that I had said to her at one time, before both of us were married that if any . . . immigrant girl could learn to cook, why couldn't I if I tried."[27] This comment is more readily understood in the context of the domestic science movement that arose during the early years of the Progressive Era (1879–1920).

Ellen Henrietta Swallow Richards is credited with founding the field of domestic science in the early 1880s. Her course in household chemistry at the Massachusetts Institute of Technology was designed to enable women to learn how to cook and manage a household. The classes were structured around her belief that "science, technology, and industry were doing a much better job of assuring the family's health and safety than most mothers could."[28] Toward that end, she wrote the *Chemistry of Cooking and Cleaning* (1881).

Social reformers intent upon bettering abysmal living conditions in the nation's urban slums and dedicated to educating women, a number of whom were non-English speaking or nonliterate immigrants, about hygiene and nutrition became actively involved in the domestic science movement. It quickly expanded into both "a reform movement and a world view."[29] Proponents of this movement held a "steadfast middle class perspective," believing that schools could best help prepare women for jobs as domestic servants or cooks, as well as for their "natural" vocations as mothers and homemakers.[30] These activists staunchly maintained the conviction that scientific information about health and nutrition should be disseminated to the individuals normally in charge of those areas of the home and kitchen, thereby improving the quality of life for everyone.

Cooking school manuals, such as *Mrs. Lincoln's Boston Cook Book* (1884) and *The Boston Cooking School Cook Book* (1896), reflected the terribly American propensity toward the professionalization of different kinds of jobs, domestic or not. According to Laura Shapiro, after the establishment of the Boston Cooking School in 1883, newspapers and magazines gave ever-increasing space to recipes and cooking tips.[31] There was also a strong belief that educated, literate women could learn the basics of housekeeping, sanitation, and cooking within a six-week period.[32]

Mrs. C. F. Moritz, with coauthor Miss Adèle Kahn, in the preface to the fifth edition of their *Twentieth Century Cook Book*

(1897–98) claimed, "Of late years cooking has come to be regarded as a science no less than as an art, and in the preparation of the recipes that we here with submit, the most scientific methods have been employed. In addition every recipe has been subjected to many careful tests, and if directions be accurately followed, success in the preparation is assured. We have also endeavored to bring our recipes within the scope of the most moderate income, and in many cases where elaborateness is called for, we have given another simpler recipe for the same dish."[33]

By the time Irma began organizing her recipes in 1951 with an eye toward their publication, she had decided that "cooking . . . is an art. There is much more to it than the fire. [It is] converting of raw materials into enjoyable edible and 'healthful food.' . . . And it is more than art. It is a health measure."[34] A number of years later, she elaborated on this statement: "Cooking appealed to me. I could see both its artistic and its scientific side, and how food properly prepared and presented could lend, yes even joy, to existence, and to the lives of those about one—You were a cook, who never wasted a bread crumb, yet [you] were always liberal with the raisins in the pudding and the vanilla in the cake."[35]

ℒEAVENED BREADS AND CAKES

Irma's mother, Betty, a professional seamstress in Heddern-heim, her home village outside Frankfurt am Main, was known for her superb cooking. So naturally Irma turned to her for culinary lessons right before her marriage in November 1898. Many years later, Irma recalled that "Mamma was an excellent and interesting cook. . . . Mamma never wasted a minute. She sewed beautifully, baked wonderful bread and the best coffee cake that ever was, much better than the aunts baked, with more raisins in it, her cooking was the best in the family, except Aunt Molly's who ran her a close second."[1]

Standing directly at her mother's elbow in the kitchen, Irma probably would have watched as Betty prepared some of her traditional receipts. Perhaps Irma had asked to learn how to make her own favorites, or maybe she was trying to collect instructions for a number of different dishes so she could vary the meals she would soon fix for her husband. She translated these recipes into English as her mother worked because "Mamma and Aunt Rose, the 2 youngest of the [7] sisters . . . [had] wanted to go to night school to learn English, but people laughed at them. Everybody spoke German. They regretted all their lives that they allowed themselves to be influenced."[2]

Some of the dishes Irma recorded in her "First Cook Book" mixed English with phonetically spelled German; they also lacked complete instructions. These points strongly suggest that she was neither copying them from a book nor attending formal culinary classes but was taking quick notes while translating, apprenticed at the side of a "master" cook—much as countless generations of young girls and women had done before her. They epitomize what has been called the art of cookery, creativity in the kitchen that requires neither science nor scientific measurements to be legitimate.

The lack of written detail about pan preparation, oven temperature, baking times, and doneness tests implies Irma was working alongside her mother as Betty mixed, cooked, and baked the various dishes. An experienced cook knew just when the look, feel, smell, and taste of whatever she was preparing was correct; a literate novice learning from that kind of cook most likely would write down the words exactly in the order they were spoken. That same novice would have acquired competence first by observing, then by working through the required steps, and, finally, by practice.

Many of the receipts Irma jotted down were for cakes and breads. At first glance, this might seem unusual, especially for a young woman who needed to learn the basics of meal preparation, but Germans traditionally placed these kinds of comestibles high on their list of important foods. Along with coffee or other beverages, they were the main ingredients of a good, solid German breakfast, an afternoon get-together, or a light supper. The Max Kade Institute in Milwaukee finds:

> While cake in America is mostly served as dessert, in Germany it is the basis of a special meal that serves a distinct function in social interactions. . . . Germans who immigrated to the United States brought their coffee-and-cake tradition with them. The importance of it is reflected in the German-American cookbooks. Not only do the cookbooks include an abundance of recipes for cakes, cookies, tortes and homemade choc-

olates, but also special chapters on *Kaffee- und Theege-sellschaften* [coffee and tea parties]. In these chapters the German immigrant *Hausfrau* [housewife] is advised on how to properly entertain at a coffee or tea party, how to set the table, what cakes to serve on what occasion, how to decorate the room, etc.[3]

Esther Levy's *Jewish Cookery Book* (1871) provides yet another level of meaning for cakes and cake making by paraphrasing Genesis 18:6: "From the days of our mother, Sarah—when her husband bids her 'make cakes' for his celestial guests—Jewesses have not distained [*sic*] attending to culinary matters."[4] As such, bread and cakes had both a special historic and symbolic importance for Jewish women. Their preparation became almost a sacred obligation—a necessity they had to learn, and to learn well, in anticipation of managing their own households and feeding their families. In addition, Irma mentioned in her memoirs that early on she had resolved that, once she had charge of her own home, she would always be "very careful that no visitor, afternoon or evening caller, [would leave] my house without offering them refreshments."[5] This hospitable attitude was especially prevalent in Jewish households, where, as anthropologists Mark Zobrowski and Elizabeth Herzog claim, "to give food symbolizes . . . the friendliness of the household to its visitors. Not to offer a guest 'honor' in the form of food . . . would be the equivalent of a rebuff."[6]

As part of her efforts to become a good hostess and homemaker, Irma also copied instructions for making coffee from a newspaper column. It was the single beverage that most often accompanied morning and afternoon sweets in German households. Although today, home roasting of coffee beans is practically unknown, it was considerably more common at the turn of the century, "as common as scrambling eggs."[7] With imported beans selling for approximately fourteen cents per pound in 1898, almost an hour's wage for the worker, coffee was, indeed, a munificent beverage that indicated a sincere effort to provide guests with something special.[8]

For the best cup of coffee, brown it and grind it at home, and always use a choice variety. If you have a roaster it is easily done, or it may be browned nicely in a moderate oven in a dripping pan. Grade the amount, of course, to the number of cups you want. Wash your eggs before using them and save the shells to settle the coffee with. An even teaspoonful of coffee for each person is a good rule.

No doubt the following receipts for bread torte and bread pudding were family favorites; they were among the first Irma recorded into her own notebook. Loaded with chocolate, sweet butter, spices, and sometimes soaked in wine, they would have provided Betty with opportunities to demonstrate her creativity and baking acumen. The lack of indicated oven temperatures and baking times might appear unfathomable to a modern cook but is understandable if one recalls that Irma was observing how long her mother let the oven heat and to what temperature and how the cakes would look when they were precisely right. Despite the profusion of ingredients and the relatively high cost of imported spices and baker's chocolate, *Brot tortes* and puddings actually reflected typical Germanic thriftiness because they called for stale or leftover bread, which otherwise might have gone to waste.[9]

Brod Tort

9 eggs
1 1/2 cups sugar
3 bars chocolate
1 cup bread
little ginger
1 teaspoon cinnamon
almonds

bake in slow oven
Pour little wine over when cold.

Brod pudding [no. 1]

Soak white bread—squeeze & add
2 eggs
sugar
cinnamon
salt
almonds
little lemon
fat or butter

put fat in pot & bake.

Brod pudding [no. 2]

Soak the bread then squeeze out water. Mix with it
1 egg
shovel & a quarter sugar (size of our shovel)
little cinnamon
little salt
little pat of butter about size of a tablespoonful

put mixture into pot with fat or butter in bottom
put in oven for about an hour.

Next, Irma jotted down a rather large number of receipts for the "fancy" cakes she wished to master. Betty must have learned how to make them herself at some point after her arrival in the United States because they employed American measurements and products not evident anywhere in her identifiably traditional European or European-based recipes. The single ingredient common to these newer receipts was baking powder, alternately called yeast powder. An advertisement for Babbit's Best Baking Powder in the National Baptist Christian weekly *The Examiner* (December 9, 1897) implies that the products were one in the same, just marketed under different names. Ostensibly written by B. T. Babbitt, who had actually died in 1889, the text maintains he was "the originator of yeast or baking powder in 1849." Isabel D. Bullard of the School of Domestic Arts and Science of Chicago described the powder scientifically in 1904, explaining how it works: "Yeast powder, as the American preparation was called, was a mixture of an acid and an alkaline powder—the former calcium phosphate and the latter bicarbonate of soda and potassium chlorid. When duly mixed with the dough these were supposed to give off carbon dioxide as effectively as yeast."[10] Yeast powder was simultaneously marketed with baking powder from 1891 to 1893 according to Chicago grocery advertisements. One-pound tins of both yeast powder and baking powder cost twenty-five cents during that period. After 1893 grocery ads only mentioned baking powder. Using prepackaged yeast powder, or baking powder, was quicker than making regular yeast from scratch and promised faster results than waiting for yeast to work. This convenience would have appealed to a "modern" woman or to a cook pressed for time, possibly leading her to spend money on packaged goods.

In Irma's cookbook, an incomplete, handwritten receipt for a jelly roll (that contains no jelly) includes yeast powder as one of the ingredients. This alone places its origins in America rather than Europe, where yeast powder was called baling powder, and the likely time frame for the recipe somewhere during the early 1890s, well after Betty had immigrated to the United States.

Jelly rolls

Three eggs, one cup of sugar, one cup of flour,
One teaspoonful of butter, one teaspoonful of yeast
  powder. Roll very thin.

Light and airy confections called sponge cakes are made by whisking together egg yolks and sugar, then adding flour and other ingredients. Modern recipes for cream sponge cake do not often call for actual cream, but Betty's receipt did. A single recipe given by J. Croly in *Jennie June's American Cookery Book* does too, and one is left to wonder whether the origin of this recipe is European or American.[11]

When she ran her own household, Irma applied techniques for making her mother's sponge cakes to whipping up that delectable, quintessential American dessert: angel food cake.

Spongue cake

7 eggs
1 cup sugar
7 tablespoonsful flour
1 1/2 teaspoonsful baking powder.

Cream Sponge cake

1 cupful powd. sugar, 1 cup flour, teaspoon baking powder, 3 eggs, one half cup full whipped cream added last thing.

In sharp contrast to the relatively loose instructions for making her mother's cakes and tortes were the newspaper and magazine recipes Irma saved. These led the cook through a systematic process. The instructions gave visual and physical property clues, so the cook could not possibly err.

Maple Sugar Cake

For the layers use one cupful of butter, two of sugar, three of flour, four eggs, one cupful of milk and a teaspoonful of baking powder. Bake in circular tins. For the filling, boil one cupful of maple sirup until it threads, and drop into it, little by little, the well-beaten white of an egg. Stir finely chopped nuts through the icing. Spread between the layers and over the top. Decorate with perfect kernels if desired.

Maple Sugar Filling for Cake

Put one pound maple sugar in a saucepan with one cup cold water over the fire, cover and boil till the sugar, when a little poured into ice water, can be formed into a firm ball; beat the whites of five eggs to a stiff froth; remove the sugar, let cool off one minute,

then slowly pour it into the beaten whites, while beat-
ing constantly; continue to beat till cold. This may be
put between the layers of cake and also used as icing
on top of the cake. For the latter spread the meringue
over the cake and set it in a cold oven until firm; it
should dry more than bake; fine chopped hickory nuts
or pecan or chopped almonds may be mixed with the
meringue and put between layers of cake.

It is impossible to say where Irma found the following recipes for caramel cake and caramel icing. They may have come
from separate sources, since the cake requires one half cup butter but the icing calls for "butter [the] size of an egg," a visually
estimated amount that was common before domestic science
mandated otherwise. It is also possible that they came from the
same source because early recipe writers, newspaper colum-
nists, and cookbook authors were not necessarily consistent in
how they presented their recipes. They often lifted recipes and
their accompanying directions from a variety of places without
additional editing to update them to more modern conven-
tions. Irma too showed inconsistency in recording proportions,
sometimes writing "teaspoon" or "tablespoon," often adding "ful," and other times simply writing the measurement as
"spoon." On occasion she even omitted the measurement words
altogether or failed to change old-fashioned words like "tumblersful" or "butter the size of an egg" into their more modern
equivalents.

Caramel cake

1/2 cup butter—creamed
2 cups sugar
yolks of 3 eggs
juice & rind of 1 lemon
2 cups flour
2 level spoons baking powder
beaten whites.

Caramel icing

2 cups dark brown sugar
1 cup milk or cream
butter size of an egg

boil till it hardens in cold water. Pour over cake while
hot.

Irma clipped a few undated recipes from newspapers and
women's magazines for sweet desserts other than cakes. Interestingly, she chose to record one for a cake and its accompanying
frosting that called for almost four ounces of imported chocolate. Chocolate was expensive, and Irma always paid attention
to cost. So why did she list these particularly extravagant recipes
in addition to her mother's chocolate-laden *Brot torte*? Maybe
she wanted to expand her culinary repertoire beyond the confections that her mother could teach her to make. Perhaps she
just liked chocolate. It was, after all, so temptingly advertised
in contemporary women's magazines, such as *Harper's New
Monthly.* Or possibly it was because chocolate's nutritional benefit, a topic that interested Irma greatly, was frequently in the
news during the late 1800s. An avid reader, Irma could hardly
have missed this information.

Famed nutritionist and dietary researcher W. O. Atwater
had called chocolate a "food appetizer" as far back as 1887,
recommending it as a digestive aid. Atwater's work reaffirmed
Dr. Jonathan Pereira's conclusions of a quarter century earlier.
Pereira claimed, "in its pure state it [chocolate] is a very concentrated and nutritious, as well as agreeable food. As such it
is much used by invalids."[12] And, as Irma mentioned following
the birth of her first child, it was also a foodstuff that her aunts
recommended highly for nursing mothers.

Chocolate cake

Dissolve two ounces of chocolate in five tablespoonfuls of
boiling water. Beat half a cupful of butter to a cream, and

add gradually a cupful and a half of granulated sugar. Beat the yolks of four eggs; add them to the butter and cream; then add the melted chocolate, half a cupful of milk and a cupful and three-quarters of flour; then give the whole a vigorous beating. Beat the whites of the eggs to a stiff froth; stir carefully into the mixture; add a teaspoonful of vanilla and a heaping teaspoonful of baking powder. Mix quickly and lightly, and bake in a moderate oven.

Chocolate frosting

4 white eggs [egg whites]
1 cup powd. sugar
1 1/2 cakes chocolate
teaspoonful vanilla.

Cupcakes, baking powder muffins or biscuits, and corn-meal-based breads were not typical German fare, yet Irma also included them in her cookbook. A "cup cake," written with a separation between the words, did not necessarily mean a small-sized cake—although it might. The name was derived from the eight-ounce cup, a British and American volume measurement, that was used to measure the amount of flour needed. This was a departure from the Germanic method of measuring by weight.

The resulting sweet morsels were closer in consistency to bread than to the texture of a modern cake. These quick-bread recipes Irma copied also called for baking powder to assist in raising the dough, an addition that permitted immediate baking. Cupcakes were fairly simple, effortless, and straightforward. They were also versatile because they could be served with either coffee or tea for a snack or as a dessert.

The wording of the instructions for making the cupcakes and muffins implies they may well have been other receipts Betty had learned after she had arrived in the United States. If so, she might have gleaned them from recipes printed in one of the local German-language newspapers.

Cup cake [no. 1]

Cream one scant cup of butter with about 1 1/2 cups of sugar add gradually the yolks of 4 eggs one at a time. Sift 3 cups of flour, measure again after sifting and add 2 teaspoonfuls of baking powder in last sifting. Add alternately the sifted flour, and a cup of scalt milk. Add to the last stuff beaten whites of the eggs. Flavor to taste.

Cup cake [no. 2]

Butter about the size of egg
1 cup sugar or little more than 1 cup
5 eggs
about 3 cups flour
2 1/2 tea-spoons baking powder
1 cup milk.

Muffins

1 tablespoonful butter
1/2 cup sugar
2 eggs
1 cup milk
flour
1 1/2 teaspoon baking powder.

Corn was an American ingredient infrequently used overseas until around the 1890s, when Mrs. S. T. Rorer of Philadelphia, principal of the Philadelphia Cooking School, took the initiative to introduce maize-based dishes to Europeans.[13] Closer to home, a rather dry article published in the *Chicago Daily Tribune* mentions Mrs. Rorer's using maize in cooking demonstrations at the Women's Building at the Columbian Exposition in Chicago. She reportedly made "mush with cream of maize sauce and apricots" then planned to demonstrate the technique of making "Indian dumplings" to fairgoers.[14]

Although corn may not have been a popular ingredient, or even much known outside the United States until the nineteenth century, instructions for making corn bread and muffins appeared in Esther Levy's 1871 *Jewish Cookery Book,* the first American kosher Jewish cookbook. The recipes she included were of German, English, Sephardic, and American origin, along with some that were labeled "traditional Jewish favorites."[15] In this book, Levy, like other recipe compilers of the time, printed receipts that employed the European weight measurement system as well as the imprecise "handful" and "pinch" method. Irma's recipe for johnnycake, because it called for "a little sugar," may have been another one her mother learned in Chicago, since traditional Southern cornbread was not "fancied up" with sugar, as were versions devised for Northerners' tastes.

Johnny cake

1 tablespoonful butter
a little sugar
3 eggs
2 cups milk
3 cups yellow sifted corn-meal
1 1/2 cup white flour mixed with the corn-meal
3 teaspoonful baking powder

Given the importance Germans placed on breads, it is rather surprising that Irma's cookbook did not contain more receipts for this staple. The single recipe for loaf bread that Irma included in her cookbook came from a newspaper, most likely either from the *Chicago Record* or the *Inter-Ocean.* The *Record* ran a regular recipe column called "Meals For A Day" in which readers' prize-winning "bills of fare" and recipes were printed. In 1896 the culinary editor collected ten thousand of these into *The Chicago Record Cook Book,* "carefully indexed and substantially bound in art canvas," which was sold through the mail for one dollar.[16] The *Inter-Ocean* published daily recipes, with famous domestic scientists Marion Harland and Mrs. Mary J. Lincoln appearing twice weekly in a column called "Household Letters." Circulation figures for both these morning dailies were high. Each paper cost two cents and so provided homemakers with an inexpensive alternative to hardcover cookbooks for recipes, health, and nutrition news.[17]

This particular bread recipe called for whole wheat; it would have been similar in its dense consistency to classical Germanic grain breads such as rye pumpernickel. Perhaps it was for this very reason that Irma chose to clip it. The printed instructions were detailed and clear. Yet, the lack of precise amounts of flour needed implies the writer believed her readers would be experienced enough in bread making to know how much was "enough."

Excellent Whole-Wheat Bread

Select whole-wheat flour free from outside bran. Pour one pint of boiling water into one pint of sweet milk. When lukewarm add one compressed yeast cake, dissolved in two tablespoons of warm water, and one teaspoonful of salt. Mix and stir in enough whole-wheat flour to make a batter that will drop from a spoon. Beat well, cover and stand in a warm place (75 degrees Fahrenheit) for three hours, or until very light. Stir in flour sufficient to make a soft dough. Knead lightly until the greater part of the stickiness is lost. Mold into four or six loaves, according to the size of your pans; put in greased pans, cover and put in warm place for one hour. Bake in a moderately quick oven for forty minutes. This must be handled quickly. Cannot be molded dry, like the ordinary white bread.

Accompanying this bread recipe were instructions that Irma jotted down for making orange *marmelade* (marmalade). When served together, she would have had two major parts of a typical German breakfast. This was probably another of her mother's receipts because "marmelade" was given its German spelling, the measurements were weight-based, and the directions were spare.

[Marmelade]

Slice thinly

8 oranges

3 lemons

remove seeds and cover with 1 1/2 pints cold water
Let stand 24 hours then boil in some water until tender.
Remove from fire and let stand again 24 hours. Then weigh
all, and to every pound of fruit allow 1–1 1/2 pounds
granulated sugar. Boil untill it will jelly, put in glasses and
set aside for four weeks before using. This quantity will
make about 15 glasses of marmelade.

Irma's rationale for including a *Vollkornbrot* (whole-grain
bread) recipe in her booklet also might well have been because
she endorsed the dietetic "craze for whole-wheat flour."[18] This
fad arose out of the belief that whole-wheat grain flour was
more nutritious and more digestible than "fine" wheat flour and
far less likely to be adulterated with alum, sulphate of copper,
carbonate of lime, ground gypsum, kaolin, barley, rice flour, Indian meal (maize), oatmeal, or horse feed.[19] But Irma's motive
may also have been based on cost comparisons between whole-
wheat and white flours.

In 1898 Irma was working as a cadet (student) teacher in the
Chicago public school system, a position that paid seventy-five
cents per day, and was also earning a little extra money through
her writing.[20] Her husband to be was beginning his medical
practice already in debt to Irma's uncles who had subsidized his
postdoctoral training in Germany. Whole-wheat bread would
have been inexpensive to make since the main ingredient was
abundantly grown and processed in the Midwest, with huge
grain elevators located in Chicago. Then too, whole-wheat flour
was easier to produce than white flour; only the outer husks of
the kernels were removed before milling. It was not bolted, took
less time to mill, and so cost less than regular bread flour.

Yet, other kinds of cost factors may have been behind the noninclusion of other bread recipes in Irma's cookbook. The U.S. Commissioner of Labor's annual report for 1903 shows the average price in 1898 for a one-pound loaf of wheat bread in Chicago to have been five cents, as opposed to almost three cents for the average cost of one pound of bread flour.[21] After considering the expense of the other required ingredients (sugar, salt, milk, packaged yeast) along with the five hours of time it typically took to make bread, Irma may have calculated it would be more economical to purchase her loaves from a local German baker.

3

TRADITIONS AND INNOVATIONS

In both Europe and America, dinner was a hearty affair most often served around midday. The two menu plans Irma included in her notebook were obviously for the day's main meal but composed of many courses than would have been common in an upper-middle-class Victorian home only a few years previously. These bills of fare might have been her mother's suggested combinations that perhaps also incorporated some of Irma's favorite foods.

Menu plan
Rice-soup
Breast of veal
French potatoes
Green peas

Menu plan
Green kern soup
Cup or marble cake
Grape-pie
Chicken

Germans traditionally cooked plenty of meat dishes, and in Chicago they had no trouble finding the supply and variety they desired. By 1898 the city had become the meatpacking capital of the world primarily because the railway system connected it to both coasts. Rail lines coming into the city transported live animals to the stockyards, where they were slaughtered, then carried the carcasses to other destinations by way of refrigerated cars. One might think that beef would have been inexpensive in Chicago, yet one pound of sirloin steak at thirteen cents almost equaled a worker's average hourly wage of fifteen cents.[1]

One can almost sense how fast Betty was speaking as she relayed her directions and assembled the necessary ingredients because Irma often summarized the cooking instructions, sometimes even failing to translate all the words into English. One can easily visualize how quickly the older woman's practiced hands flew in the kitchen—chopping, dicing, mixing, tasting, testing, and adjusting seasonings. As with many informal cooking demonstrations, while she worked, Betty probably recalled certain things she really should have mentioned earlier, so Irma's cookbook contains what appear to be asides.

> Soup & chicken like other soup & veal
> Green-kern must boil about 3 hours
> Rendered butter ought to be cooked about 2 hours
> *Fleisch-brühe* [beef broth] stirred up with a little flour & water makes a good *sös* [sauce] for soup meat & such things.[2]

Irma would have paid attention to the cost and accessibility of certain foods and staples, as well as to the length of time they could be safely stored. Flour, as has already been mentioned, was low-priced. Potatoes from Missouri or Idaho cost around fifty-six cents per bushel and would keep in the cold cellar almost indefinitely.[3] Canned and tinned foods, whether homemade or commercially produced, enabled homemakers to serve foods out of season, to stock up when prices were low, and to save time.

[French Potatoes]

French potatoes—peal & cut in long narrow slices about 1/2 length of potatoes—have perfectly dry—dry with towel & fry in pan full of hot butter or hot fat.

Large-scale canning and tinning of meats, shellfish, salmon, lobster, fruits, and vegetables, a major time-saver for the homemaker, became big business during the mid- to late 1800s. A column by Thomas Buck from the *Chicago Daily Tribune* (February 23, 1953) documents the history of commercial food canning in the United States: "Between 1840 and 1850 salmon and lobster were canned in Maine and New Brunswick; oysters were packed in Baltimore, and tomatoes were canned commercially in Pennsylvania. . . . Meats were canned in Chicago in 1872, shrimp in New Orleans in 1875, and sardines in Maine in 1876. Peas were first canned in Wisconsin in 1881."

Commercially prepared canned goods were not especially expensive, as revealed by a Siegel-Cooper and Company ad in the *Chicago Daily Tribune* (October 10, 1897), which listed Hazel brand "petit pois" (little peas) at twelve cents for a one-pound tin. We do not know whether Irma used commercially canned ones or not, but the recipe could just as easily have been made with fresh peas.

[Green Peas]

Green peas—boil in water (pour off juice in can) little parsley when done little flour & water mixed in to paste. [P]ut peas on with water but not too much water—then after boiling—serve with tomatoes, lettuce.

Irma must have been aware of the amount of time and effort involved in preparing and serving nutritious meals. She wrote down three receipts for one-pot dishes that were easy to assemble and would have freed up a few hours in her day.

Meals cooked in a single stockpot, in a Dutch oven, or in the new slow-cooking Aladdin oven were real time-savers for women who typically spent more than forty hours each week tending to household chores. While the food was cooking, they could be working at other tasks, taking a few moments every now and then to check on the dish's progress. Dutch ovens could also double as containers in which breads and cakes might be baked.

The Aladdin oven, or "cooker" as it was also called, had been invented during the late 1880s. A sawdust-lined box with water-filled copper coils, it was heated by an electric bulb that raised the interior temperature to the point where it was possible to bake breads and cakes and to slow cook one-pot dishes. Hyped as a benefit to all women, it was supposed to emancipate them from the kind of constant stove supervision that contemporary cooking often required. Edward Atkinson, the oven's inventor, touted its advantages over the traditional stove in a series of widely publicized articles.[4] Almost immediately, several domestic scientists, Ellen Richards among them, picked up on this oven as a clever way for working women to make home-cooked meals even when they were away during the day. Unfortunately, the oven never really caught on, not because it did not work or because the foods baked or cooked in it did not taste good, but because of its twenty-five-dollar cost. So stockpots and Dutch ovens retained their popularity as the kitchen tool of choice for one-pot meals.

[Stuffed Breast of Veal]

Breast of veal—little fat in pan, vegetables, salt & pepper. About 2 1/2 to 3 hrs.

Dressing—soaked bread, salt, pepper, parsley, 1 egg. Thicken [breast of veal] gravy with flour paste.

Eingedämpft Fleisch [Pot Roast]

Let fat get hot

Put in meat & let it grow brown on one side; then turn & let other side brown.

Put in sliced onions, little celery, little carrots & let it boil. If meat cooks slowly no water is required. If it cooks fast one must add water. When tender thicken gravy with flour & water.

The edible organs of beef or veal, that is, the gut, tongue, gizzard, stomach (tripe), intestines (sausage casing), pancreas and thymus (sweetbreads), and liver were inexpensive. Irma snipped the following recipe in 1899, perhaps in an effort to add variety to her meals but possibly too because she was planning ahead in the event someone in her family became ill. Protein-rich veal sweetbreads were considered excellent fare for the sick and convalescent, the care of whom traditionally fell to the adult woman of the house.[5]

Baked Sweetbreads

After washing the sweetbreads, which should be large and white, let them stand in warm water for a little more than an hour, then plunge them in boiling water and let them simmer for ten minutes. Drain them and wipe dry, then dip into beaten egg, then into breadcrumbs, and again in egg and again in breadcrumbs. Put them in a buttered pan, sprinkle with pepper and salt, pour a little melted butter over each and let them bake in a moderate oven half- to three-quarters of an hour. Serve on hot buttered toast with pan gravy.

Although Irma's mother provided her with directions to make pan gravy, Irma turned to a newspaper for instructions on how to make the white sauce that would dress up plain dishes or make leftovers taste "new." According to Laura Shapiro, gravy was commonly made with two tablespoons butter, two tablespoons flour, and one cup milk.[6] Irma's adapted selection, which includes possible uses for the sauce, reads:

Cream sauce

Get some milk, a little butter, pepper & salt—grow hot; then add flour enough stirred in milk to thicken & boil for a few minutes. (Add this to the yolk of an egg stirred with a little milk if desired.) Pour over asparagus or anything else. Little baking soda put into sauce for Lobster-a-la-Newberg when cherry-wine is added, or into cream-tomato-soup before mixing the soup as prevents the milk from curdling.

Many different varieties of vegetables were seasonally available locally from farms just outside the Chicago metropolitan limits, as well as from backyard kitchen gardens within the city. Besides peas and potatoes, Irma's cookbook contains specific recipes for only two other vegetables: celery and spinach. Perhaps she planned to use other vegetables solely as additives in soups and stews or as flavoring ingredients, as with onions, rather than as individual accompaniments to main courses.

Celery was grown in Celery Flats near Kalamazoo, Michigan, as well as in California. It was available in Chicago almost year-round at little cost. Weekly wholesale reports during 1898 show the price of California celery held fairly steady at between forty and fifty cents per dozen bunches. In May, when local crops of this vegetable began to appear in Chicago markets, the price of "homegrown celery" was fifteen to twenty cents per dozen.[7] One newspaper columnist touted Midwest spinach as "the only fresh vegetable to be had at a moderate price."[8] A frugal homemaker would have been wise to learn how to prepare these particular vegetables in as many ways possible.

One news column discovered in Irma's notebook contains a long discussion of cooked celery recipes. It heralds the nutritional benefits, tells how to prepare the vegetable in a variety of ways, and provides clear instructions for cooking. It may be that Irma cut this column because in addition to being available, celery was versatile; it could be served in a cream sauce, in stock, with meats, poultry, or shellfish, or in salads.

Celery
Cooked celery is a healthful and savory vegetable and it is too infrequently served. The native celery is not in its prime at the present, but California celery is now in market and it is excellent when cooked. . . . Celery

can be stewed in two manners, in cream and in stock.
Wash and scrape the white part of two heads of cel-
ery. Cut them in inch pieces. Cover with boiling water
and simmer gently for half and hour. Season with salt.
Add a pint of cream sauce.

Celery stew in stock—Prepare as for creamed celery
and simmer half an hour in one pint of stock. Mix
together two tablespoonfuls of butter and one of flour.
Stir this with celery. Season with salt, and simmer five
minutes longer.

Celery au jus—Cut heads of celery into pieces six
inches long, leaving them attached to the root; remove
the coarsest branches and trim the roots neatly. Par-
boil it for five minutes. Make a brown roux, using two
tablespoonfuls each of butter and flour, one teaspoon-
ful of salt, and one-quarter teaspoonful of pepper. Add
two cupfuls of stock when the roux is well browned;
and in this, place the branches of celery; cover and
cook very slowly for twenty-five minutes. Remove the
celery and place evenly seven on a dish. Strain the
gravy and pour it around or over the celery.

Irma's receipt for making spinach was basic, yet tasty. The
wording strongly suggests that she translated her mother's fast
German instructions while observing the preparation.

Spinnage

After the spinnage has boiled, been squeezed out &
chopped[,] let it alone till you have cut up some onions
fine and have let the onions fry in a goodly amount of fat;
to the fat & the fried onions add flour & when the stuff is
yellow put in the chopped spinnage, fill up with soup or
plain water, add pepper & salt & then let the whole thing
come to a boil.

Meat-based soups and stews, favored fare for colder weather,
used less expensive cuts of beef. Large quantities could be made
at one time, stored in an icebox, then reheated. If a big pot of

soup were made at the start, it could be served over a number of days, thus saving the cook many hours that normally would have been devoted to additional meal planning, shopping, and cooking. Yet, despite time-saving inventions, along with soups and stews in her repertoire, food preparation, cooking, and serving continued to be labor-intensive tasks with which Irma typically struggled. Indeed, as late as June 17, 1937, she noted, "I believe, tho, that Ruth [daughter] is right about my being too *abgehetzed* [wearied to the point of complete exhaustion] at the time of serving meals, I must try to change that—probably it is a matter of not taking enough time to prepare and serve meals."[9]

[Rice Soup]

Soup meat cut up in fairly large slices, cut off fat, put in celery, carrots, tomatoes & fill up with water. Let boil about 3 hours, strain. *Schaum* [take foam] off top & strain all when done. Boil rice & add to soup, put in flour & water if not thick.

Other kinds of soups could be made without meat. These would have used low-priced wheat, fresh or canned vegetables, and dried beans. The green kern soup for which Irma simply noted "boil about three hours" was not made from corn as the name seems to imply. Instead, it was made from toasted or roasted kernels of green wheat, cooked much as one would make barley soup. Green kern soup was a traditional Jewish dish as well as a favorite European one. It may also have been symbolic, since the main ingredient, roasted grain, most likely dried and roasted green durum wheat, *Triticum durum* L., is mentioned in the Bible seven times.[10]

Peas soup

soup beans—put on with salt water[;] when soft add little vinegar, sugar, lemon, thicken with flour & water.

Vegetable soup

Cut up vegetables & let them boil—put potatoes in last after the other stuff boiled. Little fat, flour & salt.

Chicago cooks had almost unlimited access to fish from the Great Lakes, even during the winter months. By the 1880s, the Great Lakes fishing industry was a huge commercial enterprise.[11] Pickerel, lake trout, perch, whitefish, herring, pike, bass, smelt, and government-stocked carp, also found in the Illinois River, were only a few of the readily available varieties.[12] With the advent of refrigerated rail cars, freshwater and ocean fish were packed in ice, then shipped throughout the United States. According to historian Barbara Krasner-Khait, "The increasingly widespread distribution of fresh foods expanded markets and helped to create healthier diets of meat, produce, eggs, butter, milk, cheese and fish."[13]

During the heyday of commercial fishing, prices were kept low through stiff competition. Fishmongers were abundant throughout the city, and it was even possible to purchase small quantities of fish right off the boats down at the confluence of Lake Michigan and the Chicago River. Reflecting this local plenty, and perhaps mindful that fish was a traditional Jewish symbol of abundance and fertility, Irma recorded what appear to be Betty's recipes. Both the *Suz-und-Sauer Fische* (sour fish) and *Limone Fisch* (sharp fish) receipts, with accompanying sauce (*soße*), were typical German fare hailing from the Frankfort region but were also found elsewhere in cuisine from central Germany. Another indication that these were probably dishes Irma's mother taught her is that they included German celery. Celeriac was never popular in the United States, but German cooks frequently used this turnip-rooted vegetable, primarily in soups and stews.

Irma's seafood recipes required only "firm fish," although Germans may well have preferred to use carp. To make the following boiled fish recipe, however, Irma indicated "white fish" was needed.[14]

Fish

Salt fish for about 2 hrs.
Fish with lemon *sös* (white fish)
Put on to boil
German celery
Onion
Carrots
Water

When boiling add fish & enough water to cover fish. Put head & *Schwanz* (tail) on bottom so that they will burn first if anything wants to burn. Let this stuff boil for about 3/4 of an hour.

Sour fish

2 ginger snaps
1 large onion
water, let boil
raisins
1/2 lemon, little vinegar and sugar
let all boil

fish must be salted, then salt washed off. Let fish boil in the sauce at first quick, then slowly. Let boil about 3/4 of an hour.

Sharp fish [no. 1]

Parsley, onions, celery,
All kinds of green stuff
Little butter in the sauce & little flour
1 or 2 drops of lemon or vinegar, pepper & ginger in the sauce

put in fish & boil quick first, then boil slowly 3/4 of an hour strain sauce & stir up with yolk of an egg.

Sharp Fish [no. 2]

Boil same as above except to put no butter or flour in the gravy. Take fish out of gravy & serve with melted butter poured over.

Sös

Juice of one lemon
3 yolks of egg
little parsley
teaspoon mustard
teaspoon corn starch stirred in little water
1/2 teaspoon sugar

mix with cold sauce of fish strained then put mixture on to boil stirring constantly till it boils up—then let the whole thing grow cold & pour over the fish.

Irma, in her efforts to learn whatever she could about a specific subject, cut the following food column that dealt with fish from the *Ladies' Home Journal*. She clipped so closely that she cut off the date, but, like all the other recipes she amassed from magazines and newspapers, it most likely appeared between 1898 and 1899. The segment she saved concerned general information about baking fish, then gave recipes for a baked fish dish accompanied by a zesty tomato sauce, as well as for a simple, breadcrumb-coated scalloped fish.

As for boiled fish, a general rule will cover all kinds of baked fish. After the fish has been scraped free of scales rub into it one tablespoonful of salt. Stuff the fish with a mixture made of a large tablespoonful of melted butter, one cupful of dried bread crumbs, one teaspoonful of chopped onion, one of chopped parsley, salt and pepper to taste, and fasten the fish with skewers. Butter a tin sheet and put into a baking pan. Cut gashes across the fish and lay in them strips of pork. Dredge well with salt and pepper. Cover the bot-

tom of the pan with hot water. A fish weighing five pounds will require one hour's baking. The fish should be basted every fifteen minutes. Tomato sauce is an excellent addition to baked fish. One quart of canned tomatoes, two tablespoonfuls of butter, two of flour, eight cloves and a small slice of onion. Cook the tomato, onion and cloves ten minutes. Heat the butter in a small frying-pan, and add the flour. Stir over the fire until smooth and brown, and then stir into the tomatoes. Cook two minutes. Season with salt and pepper, and rub through a strainer fine enough to keep back the seeds.

Scalloped Fish

Remove the bones and skin from cold cooked fish and separate it into flakes. Butter a pudding dish, put in a layer of fish, then one of breadcrumbs and season with butter, pepper and salt. Alternate the layers of fish and crumbs until the dish is nearly full, then pour over the whole one cupful of rich milk to which two well beaten eggs have been added, and bake a nice brown.

Slipped among the pages of Irma's notebook were also a few recipes calling for oysters, decidedly nonkosher shellfish. Although she had been raised in her grandfather's Orthodox Jewish home following her father's death when she was young, she, like any number of other Reform Jews, did not keep kosher when she ran her own home. As a case in point, one contemporary Jewish author, Bertha Kramer, in her 1889 *"Aunt Babett's" Cook Book: Foreign and Domestic Receipts for the Household* included recipes for oysters, shrimp, and ham.[15] Barbara Kirshenblatt-Gimblett notes:

> *Treyf* (unclean, non-kosher) cookbooks like that of "Aunt Babette" reveal how Jewish identity was constructed in the kitchen and at the table through the conspicuous rejection of the dietary laws and enthusiastic acceptance of culinary eclecticism. At "Aunt

Babette's" table Jewish diners would not be estranged from their non-Jewish friends by what they considered irrational and foreign practices. On the contrary, they would display the gastronomic connoisseurship and social graces appropriate to a well-to-do elite.... Inclusion of oysters, shrimp, and ham, though not worthy of mention in a general American cookbook, make the statement, in cookbooks by and for Jews, that it is not necessary to observe ritual law to be Jewish.[16]

Even so, it is possible that Betty did not prepare oyster dishes herself and so could not share her receipts with Irma. If that were true, it would explain why Irma turned to the print medium for information about how to cook and serve oysters.

Devilled Oysters

Look over, wash, drain and slightly chop one pint of oysters. Make a sauce one one-quarter cup butter, one-quarter cup flour, two-thirds cup of milk and the yolk of one egg. Season with salt, cayenne, lemon juice, and add—if liked—half tablespoon chopped parsley, then the oysters. Put buttered scallop shells in a dripping pan and fill half full of melted butter with one cup cracker crumbs, then cover each scallop lightly. Bake in hot oven fifteen minutes.

Irma cut the following recipes for oysters from another issue of *Ladies Home Journal*. She did not save the date, but the mention of "shredded wheat biscuits" in the first recipe places the column date after 1893, when this cereal was invented.

Oysters in Baskets

For four persons at table you will need one pint of oysters. The recipe is easily doubled. Cut an oblong shape from each of four shredded wheat biscuits, lay this aside, and take out all the loose inside shreds, forming a shell. Sprinkle these with salt, pepper, and put a small piece of butter in the bottom. Pick over the oysters and divide in the shells. Season with salt and pepper; dip the covers in the liquor from the oysters and lay over the shells, put on a bit of butter and bake twenty-five minutes. Serve with white sauce made of one cup milk, oyster liquor if left, flour, butter, salt and a little onion if liked.

Oysters with celery

Place a saucepan with one pint of fresh cut table celery over the fire, cover with boiling water and boil till tender; season with one even teaspoonful salt, a quarter teaspoonful white pepper; mix one teaspoonful corn starch or flour with one ounce of butter, add it to the celery; add twelve oysters without their liquor; cook until the oysters begin to ruffle; then lay six slices of buttered toast on to a hot dish, pour over the celery preparation, having two oysters on each piece of toast, and serve. If handy, add half gill of cream.

Oysters were not high-priced delicacies during the latter part of the nineteenth century. In fact, a quart of these shellfish was approximately half the cost of a pound of top-grade beef, according to Wilbur Olin Atwater's 1888 survey.[17] They were so abundant and cheap that they were also regularly made into soup for the Chicago invalids and poor who patronized Jane Addams's Hull-House Diet Kitchen.[18] In addition, they were extolled in at least one cookbook as "more easily digested than meats," especially for children.[19] Oysters, then, brought to Chicago fresh in season by refrigerated railcars or tinned at other times during the year, would have served a number of purposes for Irma once she had established her own household. They would have been economical to make and would have provided "a judicious rotation in diet."[20] Plus, blandly prepared or raw, they would not have contributed to the all too common contemporary intestinal complaint of dyspepsia.[21]

$\mathcal{D}$AINTY DISHES

Irma included a few recipes in her cookbook that would have served as components of lighter meals—luncheons, midday repasts, and tea parties. The light meal receipts she selected from print sources were designed for thrifty households. Leftover meat scraps, including beef bits strained out of soup broth, could be "deviled"; sausages, costing between ten and thirteen cents per pound depending on variety, were made from lesser cuts of meat; and eggs were inexpensive at around seventeen cents per dozen.[1]

This kind of attention to cost and waste was right in line with what Sarah Tyson Rorer advised in her 1898 book, *Made-Over Dishes:*

> Wise forethought, which means economy, stands as the first of domestic duties. Poverty in no way affects skill in the preparation of food. The object of cooking is to draw out the proper flavor of each individual ingredient used in the preparation of a dish, and render it more easy of digestion. Admirable flavorings are given

by the little leftovers of vegetables that too often find their way into the garbage bucket.

Economical marketing does not mean the purchase of inferior articles at a cheap price, but of a small quantity of the best materials found in the market; these materials to be wisely and economically used. Small quantity and no waste, just enough and not a piece too much, is a good rule to remember. In roasts and steaks, however, there will be, in spite of careful buying, bits left over, that, if economically used, may be converted into palatable, sightly and wholesome dishes for the next day's lunch or supper.[2]

Irma began the pages of her cookbook containing lighter fare recipes with one that employed leftover meat scraps. She did not specify what kind of meat was required.

Deviled Meat

Cut a pint of cold meat into small pieces. Put a tablespoon butter in frying pan, add when hot, two-thirds cup stale bread crumbs; brown; add the meat, a half small teaspoon dry mustard, salt and pepper. When thoroughly heated add two hard-boiled egg yolks rubbed fine, stir and serve very hot with buttered toast.

Then she moved on to sausages. By the 1890s, sausages— short, thick, highly seasoned, minced meat stuffed into casings—were available premade from Chicago butchers, as Irma mentioned in her March 1957 memoirs. In fact, sausages were so popular that 123 different varieties were produced at the Chicago Union Stock Yards for local and national consumption.[3] Alongside the larger meat packer–sausage makers like Oscar Mayer, Swift, and Armour, many smaller producers, such David Berg and the Vienna Sausage companies, sold their kosher products from their own factory retail stores, while still others peddled their stock directly from pushcarts.

Surprise sausages

Cut the sausages apart and pour boiling water over them;
let them boil ten minutes. Drain and halve them, remove
their skins and coat a quarter-inch thick with nicely seasoned mash potato. Dip in egg, then in bread crumbs, and
fry a golden brown in deep, hot fat.

This quick and easy recipe, for which no particular type of
sausage was specified, may well have been another of Betty's
specialties that Irma jotted down during a cooking demonstration. Or perhaps she copied it from a printed source. The name
suggests it might have been an effort on the part of a newspaper or magazine food writer to enhance an older, possibly no-
longer-exciting recipe already known to many cooks. In either
case, the sausage likely would have been a frankfurter, or wiener,
because these were *Saitenwürstchen* (scalded/scalding sausages)
that did not require frying. Such meats were suitable for *Kartof-
felkroketten mit wienerwürst gefüllt* (potato croquettes stuffed
with sausage), traditional German fare. Whatever the source,
this dish was economical because it could be made with leftover
boiled or mashed potatoes and inexpensive sausages—plus, it
was filling.

Thrifty or savory, appetizing or filling, recipes for what
Irma called "surprise sausages" were printed in the *Chicago
Daily Tribune* columns periodically for more than fifty years.
However, the recipe names changed through time. Sometimes
they were called Sausage Surprises or Sausage Croquettes; other
times they were listed as Potato Sausage Croquettes or Potato
Sausage Surprises. The October 1, 1919, *Chicago Daily Tribune*
column "'Bachelor' Shows Them How To Cook" reproduced a
recipe for "Sausage Surprise," which is precisely the same as the
one Irma recorded. As in her version, no specific sausage variety
was mentioned.

Germans may have eaten many pounds of sausage each
year, but they typically ate few eggs except when blended into
cakes, pastries, or sweet breads. So it is somewhat noteworthy

that Irma also gathered a number of published recipes for egg dishes, which she inserted among her notebook's pages. Evidently, Germans were not the only ethnic group that failed to include eggs as part of their meals during this era. Cookbook author Fannie Farmer made a specific point to advise her readers about their benefits when she wrote, "Eggs being rich in proteid, serve as a valuable substitute for meat. In most families, their use in the making of cake, custard, puddings, etc., renders them almost indispensable. It is surprising how many intelligent women, who look well to the affairs of the kitchen, are satisfied to use what are termed 'cooking eggs'; this shows poor judgment from an economical standpoint."[4]

In an effort to solve the problem of how to inexpensively include goodly amounts of protein in American diets, W. O. Atwater had begun reporting the results of German "physiological chemistry" studies in the popular press during 1887.[5] These investigations revealed that the proteins in eggs, like those in meats, fish, and beans, were almost 100 percent digestible, provided necessary dietary fats, and were comparatively economical.[6] Such statistics greatly pleased those involved in the domestic science movement, since this objective data reinforced the legitimacy of the nutritional programs they were advocating. Irma, an insatiable reader, was undoubtedly aware of Atwater's studies, as well as of the tenets of the domestic science movement.

For the most part, Irma's egg recipes were simple and quick to make. The nonomelet ones were especially frugal, since they could be made with previously cooked eggs, as Mrs. S. T. Rorer mentioned in the tenth edition of *Made-Over Dishes*: "The soft boiled eggs that are left from breakfast will be at once hard boiled, put into the refrigerator, and when four have accumulated, use them for Beauregard eggs, à la Newburg dishes or garnishes."[7] An added benefit to the bride to be would have been that stuffed eggs, according to a 1895 news column, "Summer Dishes and Drinks," were reputed to be particularly popular with men.[8]

These egg recipes allowed little room either for a cook's innovation or for error. The author noted the main ingredients (fresh eggs, which meant they were to be less than twenty-four hours old, and good fresh butter), listed the utensils needed to accomplish the job, then provided step-by-step instructions that, if precisely followed, would result in extremely palatable egg dishes.

An interesting side note concerning the omelet recipe is that the author called for a flat frying pan, a somewhat new invention that in 1898 might not have been found in every woman's kitchen. Although cookstove design had changed to the degree that three-legged, round bottom, cast iron frying pans, sometimes called "spiders," were no longer truly serviceable, not every home had switched to the newer model. A case-knife, on the other hand, was a round-tip table knife found in most households.

The way to make an Omelet

It is surprising that a dish so easily prepared, and so delicious, as omelet, has come into use so small an extent in this country. Many housekeepers never have it upon their tables because their cooks do not know how to prepare it. Omelet is simply egg beaten and fried in butter. Break three fresh eggs into a bowl, add a little pinch of salt and a teaspoonful of water, and beat the eggs thoroughly. Then put a tablespoonful of good butter into a flat frying pan, and hold the pan over the fire with the handle a little elevated so as to incline the bottom at a small angle. As soon as the pan is warm pour in the eggs, and as the mass begins to cook run a case-knife under it to keep it from burning to the pan. As soon as the surface is about to dry fold one-half of the omelet over the other, and it is ready to serve. It can be made in five minutes and is an exceedingly delicate and delicious morsel.

Beauregard eggs

Put 5 eggs into hot water, bring to a boil, and keep just below the boiling point for twenty minutes; throw into cold water and quickly cool. Remove the shells, separate the whites and yolks, keeping them apart. If you have a vegetable press, put each through separately; otherwise, chop the whites very fine and put the yolks through a sieve. Toast five good-sized pieces of bread, trim off the crusts and put them on a heated platter. Put a teaspoonful of butter and one of flour into a saucepan; mix; add half a pint of milk, stir until boiling, then add the chopped whites and a level teaspoonful of salt and a dash of pepper. Reheat, and pour over the toast; sprinkle over the yolks carefully, dust lightly with salt and pepper, and stand a moment at the mouth of the open oven door; then serve as hot as possible.

Stuffed eggs

Boil ten eggs twenty minutes, peel off the shells and cut each egg in half, so as to form two cups. From the end of each cut a small slice so that they will stand firmly. Remove from each egg the yolk, and put all the yolks in a bowl. Mix together in an earthen sauce pan two eggs well beaten, one teaspoonful of dry mustard, three teaspoonfuls of sweet cream, one teaspoon of salt, one teaspoonful of pepper, two teaspoonfuls of olive oil and two teaspoonfuls of vinegar. Boil until thick as custard and mix with the hard boiled yolks. Fill the cups made from the whites with the mixture and set on the ice until they are cold. Arrange with lettuce leaves on a plate and serve. This is a delicious supper dish, or it can be made for a salad course at dinner.

Egg salad

Boil the desired number of fresh eggs hard. Peel, cut in halves. Mash the yolks with butter; add pepper, salt, sugar and celery seed. Mix part with finely chopped

breast of chicken and fill the cups in the egg whites.
Put in center of salad plate, either in halves or whole,
and about the edge sandwiches of thin, white bread
buttered, and with a little dressing between. Cut these
in small diamond shapes.

In 1895 the famous Chicago chef A. C. Thomas advised his readers that "the proper time [today] to serve salads is at luncheon. It is distinctively a luncheon dish. In former years, they used to be served at dinner, but, a salad is something that is never found at a properly served dinner now."[9] Growing up in a German household, Irma would have been no stranger to salads, but serving them at lunch rather than at dinner may have taken some adjustment.

Ethnic Germans made all kinds of salads using green beans, red beets, potatoes, cabbage, fish, including herring, meats like Thuringer, and even wild greens such as dandelions that they typically served at the main meal of the day. However, American salads were different. Laura Shapiro maintains that

American salads traditionally had been a matter of fresh greens, chicken, or lobster, but during the decades at the turn of the century, when the urban and suburban middle class was beginning to define itself, salads proliferated magnificently in number and variety . . . Salads were so strongly identified with the upper ranks of society that even in families employing a cook, the lady of the house was expected to make the salads herself. . . .

Salads enhanced the femininity of the whole meal and made the scientific cook herself more socially palatable. Decorative, seemingly ephemeral, salads were perceived as ladies' food, reflecting the image of frailty attached to the women who made them.[10]

But did Irma, who already belonged to the middle class, really believe that decorative salads or dishes augmented with garniture were required to signal her social position or were key to making herself "more socially palatable"? If she did, one would expect to find many recipes for them included in her cookbook. Instead, there were only a few for salads and a single set of instructions for making a garnish.

Curled Celery for Garnish

Select large heads of good celery, trim away the roots and green parts. Wash thoroughly and cut in two-inch lengths. With a sharp knife split each piece evenly about six times, leaving half an inch at the bottom uncut. Throw into ice water, which should be kept very cold. It will take two hours to curl. Attractive for salads and cold meats.

Celery salad can be dressed either with French or Mayonnaise dressing. Bits of celery left from the table can be used with equal parts of cabbage chopped fine and served with a French, Mayonnaise or boiled salad dressing, which is made of the yolk of three eggs, one-half teaspoonful each of mustard and pepper, and one teaspoonful each of sugar and salt. Beat them together, place the bowl in a pan of boiling water, and stir until the mixture becomes a little thickened. Pour this while hot over the cabbage and celery, and set away to cool.

Celery salad

Carefully wash and cut in small pieces enough celery to make a pint, using only the inside pieces, saving the outer ones for the soup; stone and chop twelve olives; take half-cup walnut meat, blanch and chop fine; put all into the salad bowl; add small teaspoonful salt, liberal pinch cayenne and half-teaspoon lemon juice; mix well together; set on ice and serve with mayonnaise dressing. This must not be made long before using or the celery will lose color.

One need only look through Irma's later diary entries for clues to how she perceived salads, garnishes, and, in truth, to how she viewed food overall. On Friday, April 8, 1938, she clearly expressed what interested her about aesthetic enhancements to food: "Decided that garnishing is no trick—Parsley, tomatoes carrots, pimiento radishes are the medium—wonderful color combinations." Further, an undated 1953 diary entry set her meal presentation philosophy squarely at odds with Shapiro's interpretation: "Many a dinner table have I set that I thought was in itself a picture, not always conventional, but always as lovely as I could make it—but the important things at a dinner party, I am convinced are the food and the guests." Indeed, Irma's outlook seems to be more in tune with an 1898 *Chicago Daily Tribune* article titled "Art In Decorating Dishes." This column appeared on the newspaper page generally devoted to serial novels, fashions, bills of fare, recipes, and other items deemed of interest to women. The author reminded her literate, middle-class, female readers that a dish's appearance and presentation contributes much to the diners' enjoyment of the food, and that "the one great art in decorating dishes is symmetry. . . . In decorating dishes always make the outside sides alike, to get a balance of color or design. Diamonds, squares, circles, fleur de lis, in fact, almost any outline can be picked out by means of powdered or chopped garnishes, while, of course, the possibilities of the caper and the olive are endless."[11]

Contemporary domestic scientists were not only engaged in developing interesting recipes, suggesting new combinations of ingredients, and passing along cooking methods but were also vitally concerned with nutrition and health. Whenever possible, their writings mentioned the most up-to-date thinking about the health-related benefits of different kinds of foods. For example, another article in the *Chicago Daily Tribune,* titled "Dainty Summer Salads," gave instructions for preparing celery, then noted its "well-known value as a nerve-builder." A regularly run half-page advertisement for a "Spring Tonic" of "celery compound" in the same paper asserted that it "wipes out unhealthy humors from the blood, opens up the skin and makes it do its full share in purifying the blood."[12] And, *The Chicago Record Cook Book* unequivocally declared, "Celery is particularly good for nervous and rheumatic people."[13]

There was a lone recipe for fruit salad among Irma's papers. It was obviously one she anticipated serving on special summer occasions because the recipe was somewhat fussy for an everyday meal.

Cherry salad

This is a novel and delightful addition to the summer menu. Stone and remove the stems from a half-pound of ripe but firm cherries. Shell as many hazelnuts as required and place a nut kernel in the center of each cherry. This preserves their form and gives an added flavor to the salad. Prepare a good, plain mayonnaise, using lemon juice instead of vinegar. Arrange the white hearts of lettuce prettily in a bowl, place the cherries in the center, and just before serving, pour over the mayonnaise.

This recipe, although time consuming, would not have been terribly costly to make. Although most hazelnuts came from either Oregon or Washington State, costing upward of three cents per pound in Chicago in 1899, they still would have been a relatively inexpensive food item because when shelled and skinned one pound yielded almost four cups of nut meats.[14] Cherries were plentiful throughout the Midwest, with Michigan leading production. Like many recipes that Irma saved, this one reflected frugality, as well as some of the expanding menu possibilities that were a direct benefit of an improved transportation system throughout the United States. In the case of berries, their low in-season price was directly attributable to daily shipping by way of two different boat lines across Lake Michigan.[15]

Irma's handwritten receipts for salad dressings lacked all instructions for making mayonnaise and only gave loose directions for whipping up boiled salad dressing. This suggests they may have been more of her mother's specialties, but ones recorded in particular haste.

Mayonnaissee

3 eggs
1 teaspoonful mustard
1 teaspoonful corn-starch
2 tablespoonful oil
1/4 vinegar
1/4 water

[Boiled Salad Dressing]

6 yolks eggs beaten
1 teaspoon dry mustard
2 tablespoons sugar
2 teasp. salt not heaping
salt spoon red pepper
2 tablespoons melted butter
1 cup cream or milk
2 tablespoons melted butter [*sic*]
1/2 cup hot vinegar

Strain into double boiler & cook till thick—
take from fire and beat till cool.
Put into cold bowl & set in cold place.
Before using mix with whipped cream

Apparently the question of how to make good mayonnaise continued to interest and engage Irma for many years. An undated entry in a different pocket notebook written during 1910 contained quite a different set of instructions for this versatile dressing.

Mayonnaise [1910]

2 whole eggs—beaten well
1/2 cup vinegar (scant)
2 tablespoons oil (full)
place over fire & continue beating till it boils once
then add

1 teaspoon sugar
1/2 "" salt
1/2 "" dry mustard
1/4 pepper white

add paprika
add 1/2 bottle whipped cream
Whole bottle cream enough for 4 to 6 eggs
Add little onion juice
if desired—Good with sour cream.

Along with recipes for heartier luncheon foods, Irma's cookbook included a few more suitable either for a light repast or for a tea party. By the late nineteenth century, afternoon tea, which had started out almost analogous to the casual daily German *Kaffeeklatsch,* had evolved into a ritual in many middle-class homes. Had the middle class been surveyed, its members undoubtedly would have concurred with the novelist Henry James, who felt, "there are few hours in life more agreeable than the hour dedicated to the ceremony known as an afternoon tea."[16]

Unlike an impromptu gathering, a formal tea party was a social occasion with its own special type of attire and etiquette connoting good breeding, refinement, and elegance, as many society column reports of teas at the homes of America's upper echelon attest.[17] Although she rarely discussed women's fashions, Irma did define the role of civility in polite society—manners that were de rigeur in social settings such as tea parties. She mused, "After all what are manners? The oil of conduct—not oily conduct, the lubricant that makes contact with others run smooth."[18]

Addressing those who entertained at home, Ella Eaton Kellogg, an influential domestic scientist and the wife of Dr. John Harvey Kellogg, a vegetarian food reformer and the founder of the Battle Creek Sanitarium, wrote about the kinds of artistic table decor that would lend grace and refinement to their parties:

A very pleasing custom consists in selecting some especial color for the decorations with which the table napery, dishes, and even the food to be served shall accord; as, for example, a "pink" dinner, with roses as the chief flower, strawberries, pink lemonade, and other pink attractions; or a "yellow" luncheon, served on napery etched with yellow, with vases of goldenrod for center pieces, and dainty bouquets of the same tied with yellow ribbon at each plate, while yellow tapers in golden candlesticks cast a mellow light over all, during the serving of a bill of fare which might include peaches and cream, oranges, pumpkin pie, and other yellow comestibles.[19]

Along the same lines, a small item that appeared in the *Chicago Record* mentioned a comparable, noteworthy, easily replicated "yellow" meal: "At a recent yellow dinner tiny growing ferns in clay pots, tied with yellow ribbons, stood at each plate.... A beautiful bank of daffodils and ferns formed the centerpiece, and the candelabra were of Russian brass, with yellow-shaded candles."[20] Although there is no evidence that Irma ever read Kellogg's advice or, for that matter, this particular newspaper report, her later diaries revealed that she sometimes prepared and served color-coordinated repasts. For example, on Tuesday, July 14, 1937, she commented, "Very nice luncheon. Doilies, china, centre piece all done in light green & white. Lovely cool effect. Menu was, melon balls with mint leaves, crab. Meat salad potato chips, home-made rolls—peach ice-cream, with caramel sauce served on meringues." On Saturday, August 1 of the same year, she recorded when company came for dinner:

> We ate on the porch. Table done in red—red doilies, red flowers, red in oil cloth, red striped glasses.
> Menu
> Tomatoes stuffed with crab meat salad Planked white fish, fresh peas, Blueberry pie al-a-mode, coffee.

Then on Monday, December 12, 1938, Irma decorated her luncheon table with "red doilies, silver tinsel candle holders, red candles, cellophane centre piece on a mirror, a rose edged in red, of cellophane and cellophane leaves, holly leaves and red berries, red cherries[,] red globes—good effect."

Tea party foods included thin slices of bread and butter, small-bite sandwiches cut into fanciful shapes, and cookies, cakes, or sweets of some sort, accompanied by a punch, coffee, or, of course, tea. In 1894 a *New York Times* food columnist wrote that

> *a delicious and substantial sandwich which may be offered at luncheon or tea is made by cutting small diamonds of bread from which the crust has been removed; these are then buttered, and on the top of each is placed a slice of cucumber, cut very thin, which is in turn spread with a layer of potted meat or game. Ham or tongue is good for the purpose, or any potted meat may be used. Be careful that it is quite smooth, and place little stars cut out of hard-boiled eggs round the edge and a little mound of grated yolk of egg in the middle. Serve on a napkin garnished with parsley.*[21]

The tea sandwich recipes Irma saved read:

Reign of the Sandwich

Fashion has approved of the sandwich—probably because it is so English. Both white and fine-grained brown bread are used, and the sandwich is either rolled and tied with a ribbon or cut in some fancy shape. Here are a few of the most popular sandwiches of the present moment;

Peanut sandwiches are perhaps the newest kind in sandwiches. Spread the thin slices of white bread with mayonnaise dressing and cover well with round peanuts that have been well roasted. Served with sherry they are delicious.

Raisin sandwiches are quite the thing to serve with lemonade or sweet punch, and are made by cutting

large raisins in half with a sharp scissors and remov-
ing the seeds. Lay the fruit closely together between
thin buttered white bread and moisten with a sus-
picion of brandy or sherry, but not enough to reach
the bread and make it soggy. Cut the bread in fancy
shapes.

Nasturtium sandwiches

White bread and butter and flame-colored flowers
compose this dish. The flowers should be fresh, have
a cold bath, be flattened for service, seasoned with a
dust of salt, pepper and mustard, and be hid between
the snowy slices. Garnish with the green leaves. It is a
pretty custom to garnish individual dishes of chicken
salad with a spray of leaves and bloom from the spicy
and fragrant nasturtium.

Between thin slices of white bread, buttered, place
nasturtium leaves, well-covered with mayonnaise
dressing. These are to be served with game, and must
be eaten soon after made, as the leaves soon wither.

Surprisingly, although these sandwiches were elegant and refined bite-sized savories, their ingredients were not expensive. Nasturtiums, packets of which cost one dime apiece, were easily grown in Chicago backyards and window boxes from seed. Loose California raisins were ten cents per pound, and peanuts were characterized as "phenomenally cheap" in one 1899 *Chicago Daily Tribune* article.[22] Yet, when women chose to make and serve these dainties, it may not have been merely the slight cost of the components that inspired their choices. Instead, it might also have been because Mrs. Grover Cleveland had recently organized a ladies' luncheon in the White House featuring nasturtium and other edible flowers.[23]

Tea party menus also included a variety of delectable desserts. One in particular that Irma saved was quick and easy to make, as well as thrifty. This meringue confection was sometimes called the "forgotten dessert" since it could be baked using the heat of a still-warm dinner oven, then left overnight without deleterious effect. The sweet's delightful proper name might even have caused this bride to be to smile when she first noticed the newspaper recipe.

Kisses

Beat the whites of four eggs to a firm froth. Stir in one-half pound of powdered sugar. Flavor with a few drops of lemon or vanilla; lay the mixture on buttered letter paper in the shape or size of half an egg. Bake until a light yellow brown; take off with a knife. Stick the two halves together.

A different type of dessert that Irma might have planned to serve when guests came to call was a smooth, rich, chilled orange custard. Some innovative food column writer titled it "A tempting dish":

Take the strained juice of six oranges, sweeten with loaf sugar, stir over a slow fire until the sugar is dissolved, taking off the scum, when nearly cold add the yolks of six eggs well beaten and a pint of cream or milk. Stir over the fire till it thickens. Pour into glasses and serve cold.

The recipe called for "loaf sugar," a cone-shaped block of refined sugar that, during the nineteenth century, was made in large, clay molds, and often imported from Europe. The recipe also required oranges, perishable citrus fruits brought to Chicago either from outside the United States or from Florida and California. Until the advent of the transcontinental railroad, certain fruits and vegetables had appeared in Chicago markets only for brief periods during the year. Unlike tincture of lemon or orange that was readily available and inexpensive, fresh citrus fruits had always been costly in the Midwest.[24] An 1875 article in *Scribner's Monthly* referred to the high price of fresh bananas and oranges but still recommended their regular inclusion in American diets:

> From Marion Harland's "Breakfast, Luncheon and Tea," we quote the following timely suggestion serve your fruit as the first or last course, at your family breakfast, as may seem right to yourself, but, by all means, have it whenever you can procure it comfortably and without much expense. In warm weather you had better banish meat from the morning bill of fare three days in the week, than have the children go without berries and other fresh fruits. . . . In autumn you can have grapes until after frost, then oranges and bananas if you desire. These, being expensive luxuries, are not absolutely enjoined by nature or common sense.[25]

Another article in *Good Housekeeping* magazine (1890) continued to advise the inclusion of fresh fruits in the diet, and was not at all sympathetic to the urbanites' struggle to secure them:

> Every breakfast table in the land ought each day to have a central dish of fruit, either cooked or in its native state. Oranges and melons, apples and grapes, figs and dates, currants and the royal line of berries, cherries and gooseberries, plums and pears, apricots and peaches, bananas and grapefruits, all are rounded in outline, exquisite in coloring and delicious to the taste.
>
> In one respect all fruits are alike. They should be eaten only when perfectly ripe and as fresh as they can possibly be procured. The unfortunate denizens of large cities may be compelled to consume them after being hawked about the streets and plentifully sprinkled with dust, but that is the price they pay for other privileges.[26]

In 1898 J. A. Latcha urged the use of eastern-bound railways to transport California-grown perishables as a means to change this situation: "Oranges, lemons, prunes, raisins, and other like products can be raised to perfection and in profusion in

California. Sugar can be manufactured in the State in sufficient quantity to supply the United States and of a quality equal if not superior to that imported from Germany. It is primarily a question of cost of inland railroad transportation whether the products of our own soil shall supply the people of Maine, New England, and the Central States with these articles."[27]

Irma amassed a few receipts for sweet desserts that for the most part called for the use of fruits readily available in season throughout the Midwest or canned at the grocery store. The prices of fruits and vegetables from all across the United States found at Chicago's local wholesale produce dealerships in the South Water Market were published daily in the newspapers, typically on the same page where recipes were printed. Irma cannot have failed to note which products were in season, available, and affordable.[28] In 1898 two-pound cans of commercially tinned blackberries could be had for as little as eight cents, while the wholesale price of fresh raspberries hovered around fifty cents per twenty-four-quart case.[29]

These fruit desserts were not served plain. They were prepared with copious amounts of sweet cream or cool rich custard, decorated with delicate lady fingers, or nestled in hollowed-out shredded wheat. Four of them required making a pie or pastry crust first. Good pastry dough is not easy to produce. More often than not, it turns out tough. Making a flaky, light paste takes practice, patience, and just the right touch. Irma started with her mother's version of basic piecrust dough.

Pie-crust

Little fat or butter stirred add one egg, a scant shovel sugar, little salt, half glass cold water, stir in flour and keep on putting in flour till you can knead the dough. Roll out & make little larger than pan because pie crust shrinks. Put in filling & put stripes on top.

She copied another recipe for pastry dough from a newspaper, perhaps because it provided the kind of detailed directions, visual clues, and precise measurements that promised success when rolling out plain pastry for pies and tarts.

To Make Plain Pastry

To one pint of sifted flour add one-half teaspoon baking powder, one-half teaspoon salt, and sift. Measure three-quarters cup butter which is cold and firm and cut half of it into the flour. Mix to a stiff dough with very cold water; it will take about one-half cup. Put in a little at a time and mix with a knife. Turn on a board in a ball, then roll out into an oblong shape. Spread on this an eighth of a cup of butter with the knife, dredge with flour; fold one side to the middle and then the other side over, fold this under and over in a square shape; pat out with a roller and then add the remainder of the butter, roll out again, when it should begin to show blisters which are inclosed [sic] air. The paste may be put away in a cold place to chill or to keep until convenient to use.

The rich Blackberry Cream receipt Irma clipped from the *Chicago Record* contained an appended notation: "For recipe not given see 'Record Cook Book.'" This was a clever marketing strategy on the *Record*'s part. Women curious enough about the "recipe not given" might well have spent one dollar for *The Chicago Record Cook Book* to find out what it was and how to make it.

Blackberry Cream

Stem some blackberries until the juice can be drawn easily. Strain and rub the pulp through a sieve. Put the juice on to boil; add to it half its weight in sugar, and, when boiling, stir into it gently half the weight of the sugar in stale breadcrumbs. These should be very fine and dry. Boil up once only, then pour into a shallow china or crystal dish; when the heat has passed off set away until cold, then pile on the top a meringue of the beaten whites of two eggs (that were left from luncheon), two spoonfuls of sugar and a cup of thick cream. Ornament the outer edge with lady fingers. Very nice.

Cream Raspberry Tart

Line a pudding dish with pie crust; then fill the dish with raspberries and sprinkle them well with powdered sugar. Roll out a rather thick pie crust, and put it over the berries, leaving the crust a little larger than the dish and not pressing down the edge. Bake in a moderate oven. Pour one cupful of cream into a double boiler and when it comes to the boiling point stir in half a teaspoonful of corn-starch moistened with a little cold milk; one tablespoonful of sugar, and the beaten whites of two eggs. When thick remove from the fire and set away to cool. When the pie is baked, carefully remove the upper crust and pour the cold custard over the top. Replace the crust and serve cold.

Irma cut out instructions for making two types of pies—again she clipped off the dates they had been published. To make the Grape Pie she most likely would have purchased the Concord variety. These were widely available at summer's end in the Midwest, either in stores or from local farmers, at a cost of around fifteen cents per basket.[30] For the Prune Pie, however, she probably would have picked up a one-pound tin at the grocer's for around seven cents.[31] The prune recipe also called for shredded wheat biscuits, and so, like the receipt for Oysters in Baskets, must be dated to some point after 1893. A single aside concerning fruit, probably stemming from the times when she worked with her mother in the kitchen, appeared in Irma's notebook: "Prunes—put on with water to cover them, add some piece cinnamon, when almost done add sugar & a little corn-starch & water & let boil for a few minutes longer."

Grape pie

4 cups grapes
2 1/2 tablespoonful tapioca
1 tablespoonful butter
1 cup full sugar
1/2 teaspoonful salt
2 teaspoonful grated orange rind
1/2 teaspoonful grated lemon rind

Slip skins from grapes. Heat to boiling and cook till soft. Let cool, then press through sieve to remove seeds. Add pulp to skins, tapioca, sugar, salt & rinds.
    Line pie plate with pastry. For top make strips of dough & lay across.
    Fill crust with grape mixture dot with butter cut into small bits.

Prune Pie

One pound of stewed prunes, one lemon added in the cooking.
    When cold drain off the juice, remove the seed and lemon, and cut each prune at least twice. Heat six shredded wheat biscuit[s], then dip in cold milk, drain, moisten with the prune juice. Spread the prunes evenly and lay whipped cream over. A fine dish.

Starting in the 1890s, large, aesthetically pleasing Gros Michel bananas from Latin America invaded the U.S. market. The late-nineteenth-century consumer paid a pittance for these fruits because of the recent commercialization of the banana industry, coupled with efficient rail and steam shipping. Because this variety transported so well, the fruits arrived at the market without spoilage.[32] By 1897 Chicago ranked as the main handling center in the world for this item, with local daily consumption amounting to 450,000 bananas.[33] Domestic scientists were quick to devise recipes using these popular, now-inexpensive tropical fruits. Irma's banana recipes reflected their local popularity and abundance.

Banana Cream

Peel the fruit and rub through a coarse sieve; add as much good—not heavy—cream as you have fruit, and a pinch of salt. To one pint of this mixture put two ounces of powdered sugar. Whip with an egg-beater until it is light. Set on ice, and when ready to serve, heap in glasses, sprinkle with blanched and powdered almonds over, and a candied cherry on the top.

Steamed Banana Pudding

Beat three eggs and one cupful of sugar to a cream, add three teaspoonfuls of cold water and two teaspoonful of baking powder sifted in with one cupful of flour. Beat well, stir in two banana sliced thin, fill cups half full; steam for one hour, turn out and serve with cream.

Banana Blanc Mange

Pour a quart of fresh milk into a double boiler and when it comes to a boil add four tablespoonfuls of cornstarch moistened in cold milk and three tablespoonfuls of sugar. Stir until smooth and thick, then remove from the fire. When cold flavor to taste and stir in three thinly sliced bananas. Pour into a mold to harden and serve cold. The sweet syrup from canned pineapple makes an excellent accompaniment as a sauce.

Baked bananas

Remove the skin and the inside pith; place them side by side in a granite baking-pan; dust with sugar, add a little lemon juice, put over four tablespoonsful of water, and bake quickly.

And then there were sweet filled cream puffs and popover cream cakes baked in the terribly American iron or tin miniature muffin pans called gem pans, their delightful round, occasionally fluted shells filled with rich, smooth, sugared cream.

Cream puffs

Melt half a cupful of butter in one cupful of hot water, and while boiling beat in one cupful of flour, then remove from the fire and cool. When cold, stir in three unbeaten eggs, one at a time. Drop quickly on tins and bake twenty-five minutes in a moderate oven.

Filling

One-half cupful of cornstarch, one cupful of sugar, two tumblersful [16 ounces] of milk, two eggs.

Beat the eggs, sugar and cornstarch together and stir into the milk, which must be boiling. Let it cook until thick and flavor when cool. Cut the puffs with the scissors and fill.

Cream cakes

Make pop-overs by the following rule: Two eggs, one cup milk, one cup flour, one-half teaspoon salt. Beat the eggs just enough to mix them together; add the milk gradually, and the salt. Stir the flour till a smooth batter is formed and then pour through a sieve to remove the lumps. Bake in gem pans. When done split open the top and fill the pop-overs with the following mixture: One pint of milk, one tablespoon cornstarch, one egg, salt, two tablespoons sugar, one-half teaspoon vanilla.[34]

For a slightly lighter finale to her proposed luncheon and tea party menus, Irma solicited cookie receipts from her mother and from someone whose last name was Friedman. In later years, cookies became one of the staples in Irma's baking repertoire. They were good for snacking, excellent end notes to a meal, and marvelous hostess gifts. Sometime during 1931, she even composed a poem about them:

Cookies

Cookies are the poetry of baking—
A big cake is too pretentious

It comes mostly at the end of a meal
Cookies are just little extras
Existing for themselves—
Festive a little—not necessary—
You have to be in a mood to bake cookies.
Thinking of children
And how life is with children
If you put frosting on them
It's like the music of children
Filled with glee, glad that there are homes
And comfortable people in them
Who bake cookies with spices and sugar.[35]

The instructions for Button Cookies and Anise Cookies called for European-style measurements, although, unlike most of the other recipes Irma recorded while working with her mother, the ingredients were separated out. As with so many of Betty's specialties that Irma recorded, no mixing or baking directions were indicated.

Button cookies

1 lb. butter (fresh)
1 lb. sugar
brandy glass of whiskey w/ 1/2 lemon
2 lbs. flour
3 eggs—little bit of baking powder
sugar, cinnamon, almonds on top

Anise cookies

6 eggs
1 lb. powd. sugar
1 lb. flour
anise seeds

The following Brown Cookies recipe was a bit different because it actually included a visual clue so the cook could tell when the cookie was ready. Although Irma listed the ingredients individually by volume, probably exactly as they had been relayed, the recipe was still not what one might have found between the pages of a contemporary commercial American cookbook. In fact, calling this confection a cookie is almost a misnomer because it turns out more like a moist gingerbread pan cake.

Brown cookies (Friedman's)

If desired leave out one white of egg for frosting
5 eggs
2 cups brown sugar
stir up well
melted bitter chocolate about 2 in. x 2 in. square
1 teaspoonful ground cinnamon
almonds & citron
2 cups flour
2 1/2 teaspoonful and a half baking powder
oven not too hot
When flour in pan is yellow cookies are done

Hosting an afternoon tea, luncheon, or dinner required much forethought and advance preparation. For Irma, though, the associated tasks never became tedious, as she relayed during one of her introspective sessions:

> I like a freshly ironed gingham apron with a big pocket in it so you can fish out a recipe or put a freshly made poem into it. . . . [T]he gingham apron stage . . . preceeds the party. It is fraught with happy preparations and planning—and finally the party time arrives and you take off your gingham apron and put on your party dress and stick a rose in your hair. . . .
> I adore parties and I'm a good cook.[36]

It is tempting to believe that once Irma married, she actually prepared all the dishes whose recipes she had so laboriously copied and clipped. However, in her diaries she mentioned only a few. For example, despite the plethora of oyster recipes she amassed before her marriage, she recorded making oysters just twice afterward—and then, they were fried.[37] Perhaps by that time they had become expensive because of the pollution of the East Coast oyster beds, or maybe she and Victor simply did not like them.

Chicken salad, green kern soup, spinach, peas, boiled and broiled fish, pot roast, sponge cake (angel food cake), mayonnaise, jellyroll, and fruit salad, however, became family favorites, appearing in her diaries time and again. Was this because they were easy as well as economical to cook? Or was it because they had become her signature dishes? As proof of how well Irma had imbued the early lessons her mother taught her about thrift, even after Victor had became a successful physician, she still practiced economy. She regularly used leftovers in innovative ways but assiduously avoided smothering them in cream sauce.[38]

5

$\mathcal{O}$F Cooking and Medicinal Foods

As a youngster, Irma had been sickly—"delicate" she called her condition. She suffered from what may well have been chronic anemia with associated fatigue, as well as from frequent infections of the antrum, which in those preantibiotic times put her in bed for weeks. She reported she had contracted diphtheria while growing up, as well as the usual childhood trio of measles, mumps, and chicken pox. Even Irma's family was not immune to one of the most dreaded sicknesses that typically affected urban dwellers: tuberculosis. Irma recalled, "Uncle Manuel . . . had come home [to Germany] to die of tuberculosis, called consumption in those days, brought on by malnutrition they said."[1] One brother had succumbed to what might have been tuberculosis of the spine; her mother was often ill of some undiagnosed complaint that periodically disabled her, and her father died of septicemia. Consequently, as Irma mentioned time and again in her diaries and memoirs, she frequently thought about health and disease, casting about for ways to forestall illnesses, for ways to cure them once they had been contracted, and for foods that promoted recovery.

Life during the late nineteenth century was fraught with danger—frequently from disease. The leading causes of death were pneumonia, tuberculosis, diarrhea, enteritis, and diphtheria. Of these deaths, 40 percent were among children less than five years of age.[2] Streptococcal and staphylococcal infections were life threatening since there were no antibiotics. Repeated outbreaks of cholera, dysentery, typhoid and yellow fevers, influenza, tuberculosis, and malaria could—and commonly did—race through the population, with each new epidemic sensationally splashed across the headlines.[3]

Medical knowledge during the Progressive Era was limited, although doctors had finally been able to connect certain microorganisms to specific diseases, develop some vaccinations, and suggest a few remedies to slow transmission. One contemporary writer claimed, perhaps in all seriousness,

> Danger is made to surround everything nowadays. The germ theory has peopled space, air, water and food with micro-organisms that threaten death or disease on every hand. . . . We go to bed and behold! There is death in the pillow. Then, again, the hiring of clothes is dangerous. In cities it has become an every-day matter to hire wearing apparel, particularly dress suits, and these suits are worn by men of all sorts, of all associations, and possibly by men who have some infectious disease. If the wearer has not such a disease, the clothing may be worn in a place or among people where disease germs will be taken away in the meshes of the cloth. Costumes for masquerades and theatricals are worse yet, for they are more especially worn by the lowest as well as by the highest, by the vicious and depraved as well as by the decent and respectable; and these costumes are rarely or never washed and are used until they are worn out.
>
> Books, too, are dangerous. Rub the finger over a clean sheet, says the *American Analyst,* and a thin streak of dirt, perspiration and skin cells is the result; once reading a volume through leaves a miniscule deposit

on every page touched, from title page to finish. Sick people leave the germs of their disease. By degrees the hollows fill up, the oil of the skin tinges the pages and the book becomes dirty. Under the microscope this detritus is nitrogenous, loose, moist and decaying. One germ introduced into it will breed and produce millions of bacteria and these will live for unlimited time in the rich soil that has been gathered from a hundred hands. It is a soil for the germs of scarlet fever, smallpox and various blood diseases. Cleanliness is not only next to godliness, but it is next to life and health, and though the germ scare may be overdone, yet it will produce good results in the hands of intelligent people.[4]

Notwithstanding scientific advancements, many illnesses remained beyond medicine's ability to treat. For those, physicians could only prescribe tincture of time, coupled with plenty of healthful, hygienically prepared meals—foods typically cooked by the homemaker. Even though she was to marry a doctor aware of the most recent medical advances, Irma cannot have failed to realize that, as a woman, the care and feeding of family members who became sick would fall primarily onto her shoulders. Although she never mentioned the foods she was advised (perhaps by Victor) to eat to alleviate her iron deficiency, Irma did collect recipes for oysters, spinach, beef, prunes, raisin and peanut sandwiches, and eggs, as well as for a dish resembling the much-hyped, anemia-curing Salisbury steak—all of which were commonly prescribed during the late nineteenth century to mitigate or eliminate that problem.

Until the advent of inexpensive newspapers, magazines, and periodicals, such as *The Home Queen, Good Housekeeping, Ladies Home Journal, The Century,* and *Scribner's Monthly,* the most up-to-date sources of information about how and what to feed convalescents were cookbooks. The pertinent chapters were variously titled "Preparations for the Sick," "Recipes Especially Prepared for the Sick," "Diets for Invalids," "Food for Invalids Under Medical Direction," and "Speisezettel für Kranke aller" (Menus for All Kinds of Sick People). Of course, the homemaker would be responsible for those meals, just as she was responsible for the daily meals, care, and well-being of all her family members: "'Family' as the unit of everyday life could not be separated from food"; nor could it be separated from health.[5]

Since Irma anticipated raising a family, or perhaps because she recalled the "indigestible" lunches she had been served in high school, she clipped an article in which domestic scientist Mary Davis discussed lunch meals that might appeal to children, both sick and well. Both food items mentioned in the article were inexpensive and known to be nutritious. Davis advised her readers:

> *Broiled chicken is a very suitable dish for children. If the chickens are freshly killed lay them in iced salted water for half an hour before broiling them. This renders the meat at once firm and tender. Children should be taught to eat the dark meat as well as the white. They will find it equally palatable if they have always been accustomed to it.*
>
> *Hamburg steak is, as a rule, found to be more palatable when made into small, round cakes. The tastelessness often arises from want of good seasoning. It should, to begin with, be chopped very fine while in its raw state, and should be thoroughly sprinkled with onion juice and plenty of salt and pepper before being molded into cakes. When the butter has got very hot in the frying pan, put the steaks in and fry brown on one side before turning and browning well on the other. Remove them to a hot platter, add a tablespoonful of flour to the butter in the pan, stir until smooth, add a cup of boiling water, or bouillon made of beef extract and stir until it boils. Season with chopped parsley or a little Worcestershire sauce or tomato catsup, pour around the steaks and serve hot.*

The recipe for Hamburg steak, because it called for the addition of Worcestershire sauce seasoning, came close to the one that Dr. James Salisbury had developed during the Civil War to combat "weak or disordered digestion," that is, dyspepsia, and later advocated as a cure for anemia, tuberculosis, and diarrhea.[6] Then, too, Hamburg steak was a traditional German dish, alternately termed *gehacktes Rindfleischas* or *Deutsches Beefsteak auf Hamburg Art,* that called for hashed meats, with the occasional addition of stale bread crumbs, and was rolled into balls, then fried.[7]

In preparation for the day when she might need to tend to ill or convalescing family members, Irma collected even more articles that listed recipes purporting to be strengthening, palatable, and nutritious. The ones she chose to save documented contemporary concerns about diseases—matters that occupied pages upon pages of the daily newspapers and periodicals. They also revealed changes in thinking about nutrition and food science, as well as medical advances. Whether Irma ever referred to these clippings when facing the necessity of preparing food for sick family members is not known.

During 1898 and 1899, when Irma was selecting her recipes, Chicago was flooded with immigrants fleeing poor economic conditions and persecution in Europe and also with soldiers returning from the Spanish-American War. Many of these troops were debilitated by a variety of contagious diseases, such as typhus, measles, malaria, and dysentery. The worst communicable medical problem, however, was typhoid fever. By 1898 the city's health officials were almost overwhelmed. Dr. Neeley of the Chicago Department of Health reported,

> not a trifling part of the duty devolving on this Bureau was the attention devoted to soldiers, enlisted for the Spanish-American war, returning from camps of rendezvous and from Cuba. Many of the men were sick or convalescing and required medical attention. . . . Seventy-six trains were thus met and 936 soldiers were furnished medical and surgical relief—768 on trains or at the stations and thence forwarded to their homes.
> . . .

Another duty of the inspecting staff was the examination and surveillance of those immigrants arriving in Chicago from New York.[8]

Perhaps because Irma's future brother-in-law had enlisted in the war, or simply because she was accumulating additional data to use in case someone in her family contracted typhoid fever, she archived the following newspaper column in her cookbook:

> *Food for Sick Soldiers*
> *Typhoid Convalescents May Here Find Edibles That Are Safe and Nourishing*
>
> *Many relapses in typhoid fever are caused by improper food. Even after the fever is broken and the patient comparatively well the strictest attention must be given to the diet. The following dishes are given with the sanction of Miss Harriet Fleming, who is one of the most successful typhoid fever nurses in Chicago. They may aid in preparing nourishment for the many soldiers who are coming home with fever or are recovering:*
>
> *Tomato Soup—One pint boiling milk, one cup boiling tomato (either fresh or canned), a bit of butter size of a walnut; one teaspoon of flour to thicken, salt to taste; one-half teaspoon of soda put in the tomato when boiling; strain out every seed.*
>
> *Spanish Cream will be greatly relished. Bring two glasses of milk to a boil, then beat the yelks of two eggs with three tablespoons of sugar.[9] Put two level teaspoons of Knox's sparkling calves' foot gelatine to soak in two tablespoons of milk; when dissolved take the beaten yelks and gelatine and stir into the boiling milk. Do not boil hard or it will curdle. Pour into a dish and stir in the well-beaten whites of the eggs. Put on ice until very cold.*

Chocolate Blanc mange

Two glasses of boiling milk, two teaspoons of gelatine soaked in one-quarter of a glass of milk. Four table-spoons of sugar. Three teaspoons of grated chocolate dissolved in the least bit of milk. Stir all into the boiling milk, put in small molds and cool on ice. Take care not to scorch. White blanc mange is made by leaving out the chocolate.

Asparagus soup

Take half a bunch of asparagus, boil until tender. Pass the tender parts through a sieve, save the water in which it was cooked and add to it one glass of milk, a lump of butter, and salt. Add the strained asparagus, let it come to a boil. Thicken with one teaspoon of cornstarch. Canned asparagus can be used.[10]

Gelatine is very nutritious and can be flavored with pure fruit syrups, Knox's pulverized calves' foot gelatine is the proper one to use, being very quickly prepared and pure. It takes time to make eggnog well, but it is very strengthening, and eggs can be taken in this form when not allowed to be cooked. As many as three eggnogs a day can be given. Beat the yelk of one egg with a tablespoon of granulated sugar for five minutes, then add one tablespoon of good old whisky or brandy; stir hard—this cooks the egg. Beat the white stiff, add to the yelk, with enough milk to fill the glass. Finely cracked ice can be put in it if desired.

Acids and sweets of all kinds must be avoided for weeks, even months, after recovering from typhoid fever.

Interestingly, although these recipes were arranged in the older style paragraph format, mixing measurement styles, all but one called for a relatively new to the market brand name product: Knox's pulverized calves' foot gelatine.[11] Calves' foot broth was often one of the first foods invalids were offered as a "restorative." It was believed to be easily digested, appetite tempting, and fortifying. Liquid when hot, it became solid when cold and was frequently used as a stabilizer for other ingredients. However, making this jelly from scratch was a messy, smelly, time-consuming process. Consequently, once powdered gelatin became readily available, homemakers adopted it enthusiastically. Knox was one brand that promised ease of use coupled with "sparkling" purity of ingredients. It was often mentioned in food columns by name.

In the past, product advertisements had occasionally appeared in the back matter of cookbooks. Still, hardcover cookbooks were relatively expensive, so not all women could afford to buy them or, if they owned them, to replace them frequently. However, with the increased circulation of newspapers, and with the proliferation of inexpensive women's magazines, advertisers could reach an expanded market on a daily or monthly basis. Their large, often full-page messages were aimed at those women who had the financial wherewithal, and inclination, to buy packaged goods. Later, food product manufacturers, such as the Cleveland Baking Powder Company and the salad dressing maker E. R. Durkee Company, offered free cookbooks, which often included recipes by noted cooking experts, to that same market segment.[12] Cooking columns frequently touted packaged foods by name in the recipes they published, thereby increasing name-brand recognition as well as sales. Sometimes they also mentioned that their recipes or household tips had been endorsed by experts. Other times the columns themselves were authored by experts, the women culinary historian Janet Theophano calls "celebrity reformers."[13] These tactics gave the messages the added weight of authority. No matter who wrote the columns, packaged goods played an increasingly significant role in shaping and modernizing American cooking practices and cuisine. By clipping these kinds of columns, Irma showed that she was in the vanguard of that modernization. Yet, interestingly, none of the recipes she handwrote ever called for a specific brand name product.

Tucked into Irma's notebook pages was a neatly folded article. The paper quality was so poor that portions had disintegrated; the remaining fragment, part of which contained the date of June 2, 1899, included a subsection titled "Some Strange Foods." It is the sole published piece in Irma's cookbook that does not have any accompanying recipes:

> "Down in our kitchen, were you permitted to visit there, you would find the bakers taking out loaves of delicious bread made out of almost any possible material other than wheaten flour. Our best breads are made from nuts chiefly, and from soy—that is, a meal of beans ground up and then thoroughly digested in salt water before it is ever cooked. Cake and bread alike are beaten up and kneaded by machinery. This is to keep out the germs; gas is pumped in to raise it in place of the fermentation created by yeast and with equal care meats, fruits and vegetable are soaked, picked and treated before they are sent to the table or offered for sale. Not an ounce of food, however, is allowed to appear from the kitchen until its appearance is such as to guarantee a welcome on any table—every soup and sandwich is prepared with a view of combating the old-fashioned prejudice against invalid diets. No repulsive-looking messes, tasteless loblollies and watery, insipid gruels are turned out to excite the loathing of delicate stomachs and fastidious palates. The day when temperance at the table was obliged to go hand in hand with rigid self-denial is over, and the new science of diet makes it possible for a chronic dyspeptic to eat as varied, delicate and inviting food, as the fat gourmand. Those who suffer from occasional attacks of dyspepsia will drop in for a week and have their meals quietly in a corner, or a twinge of rheumatism will send in an elderly gentleman for a course of corrective meals and— — —"
>
> But here the communicative young woman was called off to attend to a stream of customers who brought bottles of little saccharine tablets in place of the sugar sold in the average grocery. Soy flour, which comes all the way from China and is valuable because

it contains so small a modicum of starch was in hot demand, and yet was run close by almond flour, another preparation of ground and powdered almonds from which all the starch is eliminated.

By and by the talkative saleswoman got back to her curious customer and obligingly pointed out a shelf full of glass jars containing what seemed to be a very fine grade of calves' foot jelly.

"But it isn't, you know," she smiled. "That is jelly actually prepared from ivory because of the phosphates and bone salts pure ivory holds. It is a specialty for patients with delicate lungs, I dare say," she said.

What in the text caught Irma's eye? Perhaps it was the mention of new varieties of health foods that would enable a dyspeptic to eat without pain. Or perhaps it was that the store sold fresh-baked, healthy nut breads. She was German after all. Maybe she wanted to discuss the entire article with Victor, who would probably have known if the foods really could provide the medical benefits claimed.

A similar article had appeared in the December 1891 issue of *Century* magazine. It too concerned health foods made in a kitchen-bakery, then sold onsite. Written by Maria Parloa, one of the early domestic scientists, author of her own cookbook, and occasional contributor to women's magazines, the title was "The New England Kitchen." In this piece, Parloa recounted how Ellen Richards, along with Mary Hinman Abel, and some friends decided to rent a store in Boston where they tested recipes; at the same time they evaluated foods by their protein, carbohydrates, and fat contents. The result was the establishment of the New England Kitchen. Parloa related how the women sold the results of their experiments inexpensively from the attached shop, adding that the public response had been so great they soon added "steam-kettles and gas-tables." She continued, "The reader may ask, What are the origin and aim of this New England kitchen? Is this a charity or a money-making enterprise? It is not exactly either; its object is to cultivate a taste for good, nutritious food, scientifically prepared from the cheaper food materials. . . . Mrs. Ellen H. Richards, of the Massachusetts Institute of Technology, . . . had been interested for many years in the scientific selection and preparation of food."[14]

The New England Kitchen benefited the working poor who could secure freshly made, precooked meals for their families there almost as cheaply as if they had shopped themselves and prepared the food at home. In addition, it served the sick, who could buy nutritious, health-restoring, hygienically prepared meals onsite, as well as doctors, who could purchase meals to bring to their patients either at their homes or in hospitals. Deliveries were also made to teachers and others, such as working people or school children, who had neither the time, inclination, nor ability to fix their own food.

The article then mentioned Richards's plan to establish similar kitchens in New York, Rhode Island, and other parts of the country. This strategy received a huge boost during the 1893 Columbian Exposition in Chicago where Mrs. Richards created a New England Kitchen, also known as the Rumford Kitchen, and the Boston Kitchen as part of the Massachusetts State exhibit. In her 1894 *Report of the Massachusetts Board of the World's Fair Managers,* Richards stated:

> In the Department of Hygiene and Sanitation was the exhibit known as "The Rumford Kitchen," an outgrowth of the work in the application of the principles of chemistry to the science of cooking. . . . In order to reduce, in some degree, the expenses of the exhibit, the food cooked in the Rumford kitchen, was sold under a concession from the administration of the Exposition; but it should be understood that it was not in any sense a money-making exhibit; that nothing was cooked for the sake of being sold; and that the exhibit was absolutely a scientific and educational one. . . . The Board is confident that the results . . . must of necessity be far-reaching and tend to popularize the very great importance of the subject to which it is related. . . .
>
> [W]hile the practical outcome of the taste and relish

of the food served was shown in the fact that some ten thousand people were served during the two months that the kitchen was open. . . . The results which go to testify that this exhibit was a recognized success are already apparent. The entire plant of the exhibit was put into the experimental kitchen of the Woman's Dormitories in connection with the University of Chicago, which is now in Miss Daniell's charge, and the work has attracted so much attention that . . . the great hospital for the insane at Kankakee, Ill., already secured the services of the manager of the Boston Kitchen.[15]

It is possible that Irma's article referred to a Rumford Kitchen store in Chicago. The description of the shop with its emphasis on treating invalids by feeding them healthy foods was certainly similar to contemporary descriptions of the New England Kitchen. Or perhaps the column referred to the Diet Kitchen at Jane Addams's Hull-House. Addams's kitchen store was an integral and important part of the settlement operation she had established in 1889 to care for the urban poor. Either kitchen store would have been run according to the "science of dietetics, or what might be termed the hygiene of cooking."[16]

Irma was a friend of Jane Addams. Like everyone in Chicago, she was well aware of Addams's efforts to help the poor through her West Side Settlement House. In fact, in 1891 through 1893, shortly after Addams had started her pioneering work with Chicago's urban poor, Irma had spent many days in that same run-down area, dispensing food and succor to eastern European Jewish immigrants under the auspices of the private Kopperl Relief Agency.[17] So it is possible that Irma saved this column because it concerned her friend's work in a section of the city that she herself knew well.

The Hull-House Kitchen, opened in the fall of 1891, offered Chicago's poor inexpensive meals, including "home-made bread baked in a brick oven . . . White Bread . . . Whole Meal Bread . . . Graham Bread and Case's Health Bread."[18] The Diet Kitchen, established less than one year later, initially served the sick. A flyer indicated that "applicants are required to present orders from a physician or an accredited nurse. . . . Demonstration class in Sick-Room-Cooking every Saturday from 2 to 4 P.M. by Miss Edith Nason [a trained visiting nurse]."[19] In *Twenty Years at Hull-House*, Addams recalled:

> At that time the New England kitchen was compara- tively new in Boston, and Mrs. Richards, who was largely responsible for its foundation, hoped that cheaper cuts of meat and simpler vegetables, if they were subjected to slow and thorough processes of cooking, might be made attractive and their nutritive value secured for the people who so sadly needed more nutritious food. It was felt that this could be best accomplished in pub- lic kitchens, where the advantage of scientific train- ing and careful supervision could be secured. One of the residents went to Boston for a training under Mrs. Richards, and when the Hull-House kitchen was fitted under her guidance and direction, our hopes ran high for some modification of the food of the neighbor- hood. We did not reckon, however, with the wide di- versity in nationality and inherited tastes, and while we sold a certain amount of the carefully prepared soups and stews in the neighboring factories—a sale which has steadily increased throughout the years—and were also patronized by a few households, perhaps the neigh- borhood estimate was best summed up by the woman who frankly confessed, that the food was certainly nu- tritious, but that she didn't like to eat what was nutri- tious, that she liked to eat "what she'd ruther."[20]

In another publication, Addams reported,

> Similar in spirit [to the Hull-House kitchen] is the Hull House Diet Kitchen, in a little cottage directly back of the nursery. Food is prepared for invalids and orders are taken from physicians and visiting nurses of the

district. We have lately had an outfit of Mr. Atkinson's inventions [the Aladdin oven], in which the women of the neighborhood have taken a most intelligent interest, especially the members of the Hull House Woman's Club. This club meets one afternoon a week. It is composed of the most able women of the neighborhood, who enjoy the formal addresses and many informal discussions. The economics of food and fuel are freely discussed.

The Coffee House which is being built in connection with Hull House contains a large kitchen fitted on the New-England Kitchen plan. We hope by the sale of properly cooked foods, to make not only co-operative housekeeping but all the housekeeping of the neighborhood easier and more economical.[21]

By May 26, 1899, Addams and her Hull-House Diet Kitchen staff were planning to provide cafeteria-style "Pure Food for Pupils" at Medill High School in Chicago beginning the next fall. According to a report in the *Chicago Daily Tribune,* "The promoters of the scheme, which follow[ed] the plan adopted in Boston, hope[d] to have results in better health for the children and in stopping the sale of sweets, pies and cakes to the schoolgirl."[22] Perhaps Irma thought about this new, exciting development, recalling her own high school experiences with inedible lunches, when she clipped the article on health foods.

It is also possible that the reported interview took place in Chicago's new Battle Creek Sanitarium health food store, opened around May 7, 1899, in the city's downtown area. During its first few weeks of operation, that shop with an attached kitchen, bakery, and restaurant, demonstrated its products, gave away free samples of all the health foods endorsed by the famous Michigan Seventh-Day Adventist sanitarium kitchen, and handed out a booklet describing their "line of foods unequalled for purity and healthfulness."[23]

Would Irma have attended the opening of a health food store? It would have been easy for her to get to the downtown store by public trolley—no more than a half-hour's ride. The gala grand opening might well have appealed to the young, recently married woman. New products from a reputable company would have been showcased and made available for purchase for the first time in Chicagoland. Time-saving, precooked foods could be purchased. Perhaps she might learn some new recipes or meal combinations too.

For all the hyperbole surrounding its opening, the Battle Creek Sanitarium health food store was apparently short lived. Ads mentioning the store appeared only in the *Chicago Record,* and only on May 14, 21, and 28, 1899. Soon thereafter, grocers in downtown Chicago, perhaps to fill a gap created by the store's closing, began to advertise that they stocked a full line of the sanitarium health foods.

Thus, it appears almost certain that the article Irma clipped concerned the newly opened kitchen cum store and café connected with the Battle Creek Sanitarium. The healthful, healing foods mentioned in it included soy meal and almond flour breads, saccharin, and ivory jelly—items all permitted in, but not limited to, a vegetarian diet. Dr. John Harvey Kellogg, the sanitarium's director, was a health food advocate and a vegetarian crusader. Vegetarianism was almost becoming a fad at this time, as evidenced by the fact that no fewer than eighty references to vegetarians, their diets, and activities appeared in local papers between 1898 and 1899.[24]

The article reemphasized the need for cleanliness and science in the kitchen, and, by extension, throughout the home—all major concerns of the general public, as well as domestic scientists, of whom Kellogg's wife, Ella, was one of the most famous. It also mentioned specific foods that could help treat dyspepsia, rheumatism, lung problems, and diabetes. It even sold a sugar substitute specifically marketed to and for diabetics.

How to successfully combat dyspepsia was a major concern during this period. At one time or another, rest cures, mineral water, bland diets, homeopathy, naturopathy, avoidance of ice water, improved sanitation, the use of fresh ingredients in cooking, and better, more sanitary food preparation had all been touted as remedies for this pervasive condition. J. W. Dowling, in "Old School Medicine and Homeopathy," reported that, as recently as 1882, a medical doctor had recommended small doses of arsenic.[25] Others believed that whole-wheat flour would help. One self-proclaimed "Chicago Invalid," in an 1898 letter to the city editor of the *Chicago Daily Tribune*, begged to know where he or she might find Professor Hart's graham flour because having such would "confer a boon on a whole family of dyspeptics."[26]

Contemporary diets for dyspeptics were supposed to be simple in terms of preparation, frugal in the amounts eaten, and bland. One source recommended the use of baking powder rather than yeast in the breads that dyspeptics consumed because "the microscopic plants that accompany fermentation are not all destroyed by baking; and those remaining in the bread are, though perhaps but slightly or not at all injurious to healthy persons, certainly harmful to delicate or invalid constitutions. Indeed, to this cause some of the most painful forms of dyspepsia are ascribed."[27]

Diabetics of that era were always searching for foodstuffs they could eat. Some authorities suggested the soybean, basing their advice on European tests that had showed soy meal bread to be well tolerated by those suffering from this problem.[28] In 1878 Friedrich Haberlandt, a plant physiologist, had published the results of his extensive experiments with the soybean. During his trials, Haberlandt prepared the bean in a variety of ways: boiled, baked, mashed, ground, and in soups. He wrote that it might be "simplest to use soybeans in the kitchen in a finely ground form," then spoke of his family's home-based experiment mixing soy meal with wheat flour to make bread.[29] However, his publication had been in German. Consequently, the report was not widely read in the United States except perhaps by those in the agricultural, medical, or domestic science communities who could both read German and access foreign publications.

The soybean and its uses, other than in Worcestershire sauce, remained relatively unknown in the United States for the next twenty years. In 1898 Franklin Matthews reported on the bean as if he were the first to discover it. He wrote, "[The soy bean] is equally attractive to human beings as to live stock. It compares favorably with the ordinary bean for table use."[30] That same year also saw what probably was the first reference to soy bread flour in the American press.[31]

The kitchen mentioned in the article Irma saved obviously catered to invalids, the chronically ill, and those concerned about their health. It sold a variety of breads raised by the infusion of gas (carbonic acid) and "kneaded by machinery," suggesting that it was up-to-date with the newest scientific and industrial advancements and attentive to the concerns of domestic scientists regarding cleanliness and germs. Machine-kneaded bread would be more sanitary than that made by hand, and so would have appealed to those concerned about germs, hygiene, and purity. Too, domestic scientists considered aerated bread more nutritious and digestible than yeast breads. Since the leavening took less than ninety minutes, it saved the commercial baker valuable time. Taking less time to make meant the bread could be sold more cheaply than traditionally made yeast bread. At one time, aerated bread bakeries were to be found in New York, Chicago, Boston, San Francisco, and Philadelphia. However, unlike the British, Americans evidently did not like the product's taste, so these companies closed rather quickly.[32]

For rheumatism and gout sufferers, alcohol, rich foods, starches, sugar, and salt were proscribed. Soy meal and almond flour breads would have been allowed in their diets, though. Ella Eaton Kellogg, a strong proponent of vegetarianism, waxed almost poetic about the health benefits of nut flour breads. She devoted nearly the entire chapter on fruits in her 1893 cookbook to extolling their virtues, singling out almond flour bread, in particular, as being an excellent food for diabetics.[33]

Many vegetarians, as well as diabetics, avoided refined sugar but did use saccharin, an artificial sweetener.[34] An 1888 article titled "A New Sugar Substitute" advised:

The discovery was announced some four or five years ago, and since then the discoverer [Fahlberg] has been diligently at work striving to reduce the cost of its production, in order to make it commercially useful for the many applications in the arts for which its very remarkable properties appear to make it suitable. . . . extended experiments with [saccharine] have shown that it is quite harmless in its effects when taken internally in article of food and drink. . . .

It should be remembered, however, that saccharine has no nutritive properties, and for this reason can never take the place of sugar as a food . . . nevertheless, there is good reason for the hope that it may prove of the greatest value to those who are afflicted with certain forms of kidney disease (diabetes), in which the use of sugar must be strictly prohibited.[35]

Ivory jelly typically appeared in cookbooks of this period in the chapters containing recipes for invalids. It was produced by boiling powdered ivory in water long enough to reduce it to a gelatinous consistency, then flavoring it with various herbs and fruits, such as cinnamon, cloves, and lemons. Consumptives ate this concoction in the belief that it counteracted lung congestion. A major component of the ivory jelly compound was oil of cinnamon. Dr. John B. Murphy stated, "It has been known that oil of cinnamon was one of the most effective agents for destroying the tuberculosis germ. Cinnamic acid and the salts derived from it act much in the same way." He, along with contemporary medical colleagues, held that it could also "raise vitality, [and] warm and stimulate all the vital functions of the body." It was alleged to be an "anti-rheumatic [that also stopped] diarrhea, improve[d] digestion, relieve[d] abdominal spasms, and aid[ed] in the peripheral circulation of the blood."[36]

The saleswoman in the article took great pains to make sure the reporter realized that the foods prepared in the kitchen and sold in the store and café were not "repulsive-looking messes, tasteless loblollies and watery, insipid gruels." Most likely she was drawing attention to the differences between them and other so-called health foods that had been loudly criticized for being bland and unpalatable.

Progressive Era cooking reformers paid more attention to the ingredients in their dishes than to the seasoning. In general, they eschewed supplementary spicing, which led to the criticism that many of the recipes they devised produced tasteless concoctions. Ella Kellogg's reasoning was typical: "The use of condiments is unquestionably a strong auxiliary to the formation of a habit of using intoxicating drinks. . . . A more serious reason why high seasonings lead to intemperance, is in the perversion of the use of the sense of taste. . . . An education which demands special enjoyment or pleasure through the sense of taste, is wholly artificial; it is coming down to the animal plane, or below it rather; for the instinct of the brute creation teaches it merely to eat to live."[37] Yet, these reformers also urged women to experiment with the recipes they used—but only after they had learned the basics of choosing unadulterated ingredients, hygienic preparation techniques, and the principles of nutrition as they were known at the time. In 1894 Mary J. B. Lincoln, sometimes cited as the founder of the Boston Cooking School, wrote:

> When we know what substances we need to use as food, and the proportion of each, and how to prepare them, great care should be taken that each shall be the best of its kind, not necessarily the highest priced, but that from which we can get the most nourishment and which has the fewest objectionable qualities. We may not be able to detect all the tricks of adulteration, but we can easily learn how to select good flour, sweet butter, sound fruit and vegetables, and the name, location and food value of the different cuts of meat.
>
> Another point which should receive especial attention is the preservation of food. Science has taught us much on this subject. Care must be taken not to expose food to the action of bacteria, unpleasant odors,

or contact with unclean substances. Scrupulous neatness in personal habits of those who prepare food, and cleanliness of all utensils used, and of storage places, are no minor matters. . . .

The preservation of the body, the temple and instrument of the soul, can be secured only by observing the laws of hygiene in all our habits, especially in the choice, preparation and eating of our food.[38]

Along the same vein but emphasizing that background knowledge of physiology, digestion, and nutrition was required to be an informed cook, Ella Kellogg asserted, "The common method of blindly following recipes, with no knowledge of 'the reason why,' can hardly fail to be often productive of unsatisfactory results, which to the uninformed seem quite inexplicable."[39] In their columns and cookbooks, domestic scientists, later called home economists, alerted the middle and aspiring middle classes to new kitchen gadgets and food products that would make their lives easier. They also worked hard to teach the public about food, exhorting them to sanitize their kitchens along with their lives, to improve their diets and nutrition, and to "cook American." They even lobbied for the incorporation of household arts into the Chicago public school system curriculum.[40] Theoretically, if women followed the experts' advice, they would be able to select, cook, and serve healthy foods inexpensively and hygienically, using the most up-to-date kitchen gadgetry and packaged goods. Consequently, the reasoning went, if they followed the printed recipes step-by-step, their meals would taste the same every time, everywhere across the land, regardless of the cook's ethnic heritage or social class. For many women in America, then, immigrants and native-born alike, domestic science authorities became substitutes for a mother in the kitchen.

Irma became an enthusiastic supporter of at least some of the tenets of the domestic movement. Summarizing her credo during 1958, the period in her life during which she frequently wrote about cooking and food, she noted: "I always thought of the kitchen as my laboratory and if I had cleaning to do I told myself that the progress of civilization rests on cleanliness."[41] Much later, Irma wrote that experience in the kitchen and in life had led her to believe that "[Cooking] cannot be done well, without constant supervision, which is not work, but knowing that we need to remind ourselves . . . we need constantly to remind ourselves that we want to strive for the best of things, for often the difference between the best and the not so good is very slight. . . . Eating, especially when you are hungry is one of the most pleasure-giving experiences in [a] young life—and I daresay it is in our lives too."[42]

Breast of veal — little fat in pan, vegetables, salt + pepper. About 2½ to 3 hrs.

Dressing — Soaked bread, salt, pepper, parsley, 1 egg. Chicken gravy with flour paste

French potatoes — peal + cut in long narrow slices about ½ lengths of potatoes — have perfectly dry — dry with towel + fry in pan full of hot butter or hot fat

Green peas — boil in water (pour off juice in can) little parsley when done little flour + water mixed to paste.

\# ⚹ ⅄ ⅄ ⅄ ⅄

Green-pea soup
Cup or mable cake
Grape-pie
Chicken.
Soup + chicken like other soup +

Pie-crust

Little fat or butter stirred add
one egg, a scant shovel
sugar, little salt, half
glass cold water, stir in
flour and keep on putting
in flour till you can knead
the dough. Roll out &
make little larger than
pan because the crust shrinks.
Put in filling & put strusel
on top.

Spinnage

After the spinnage has
boiled been squeezed out
& chopped let it alone
till you have cut up some
onions fine and let the
onions fry in a goodly

Rice - soup
Breast of Veal
French potatoes
Green peas

Soup meat cut up in fairly large
slices, cut off fat, put in celery,
carrots, tomatoe & fill up with water.
Let boil about 3 hours, strain Schaum
off top & strain all when done
Boil rice & add to soup, put in
flour & water if not thick

Brown cookies (Friedman's)

5 Eggs (If desired leave out one white of egg for frosting)
2 cups brown Sugar
Stir up well

melted bitter chocolate
about 2 in x 2 in. square
1 teaspoonful ground cinnamon
almonds + citron
2½ cups flour 2½ on Oct 14
teaspoonful and a half baking powder
oven not too hot
When flour in pan is yellow cookies are done

Cup cake

Cream one scant cup
of butter with about 1½ cups
of sugar + add gradually
the yolks of 4 eggs one at
a time. Sift 3 cups of

ℛECIPES

Eleanor Hudera Hanson

They met at a local pub. Ellen Steinberg, who has a master's degree in anthropology and a doctorate from the University of Illinois at Chicago, had been invited as guest author to discuss her newest book, *Irma: A Chicago Woman's Story, 1871–1966,* at the pub's monthly book club gathering, which Eleanor Hanson was attending.

Near the end of the evening, Steinberg happened to mention that among Irma's notes and diaries was also a collection of recipes and that she was entertaining the idea of organizing these into a cookbook. After the event, Hanson handed Steinberg a business card. Though not a culinary historian, Hanson has a degree in foods and nutrition from the University of Illinois at Urbana, a master's of business administration degree from Northwestern Kellogg Graduate School, and, most importantly, had spent years in test kitchen recipe development; in fact, she was a former director of the Kraft Kitchens.

Thus the collaboration began. During their initial meeting Steinberg confessed that it had never ever occurred to her that they might need or even want to actually try to *cook* Irma's recipes. Hanson suggested that if this were to be a *cook*book and *cooking* were to be in the title, the authors might want to have some hands-on experience with the recipes.

Many of Irma's recipes were sketchy at best. Steinberg prepared and researched obscure terminology and historical context for contemporary interpretation. Hanson devised a style and consistent recipe format, then began rewriting recipes. Both cooked. They live less than a mile from each other, and many plates, pots, plastic containers, and packages were exchanged for mutual tasting and discussion. They negotiated. Hanson preferred baking. Steinberg loved soups. They flipped a coin for the oysters and fish. Luckily their husbands are not picky eaters.

The resulting recipes are intended to capture Irma's spirit. They remain "scratch" recipes and have been interpreted and rewritten to reflect an era when time in the kitchen spent cooking was still considered a noble endeavor.

Irma's recipes were challenging to interpret and rewrite for contemporary use. Like so many of us who are just learning to cook and getting knowledge and inspiration from our mothers and other family members, Irma tended to "shorthand" her recipes. Since she most likely watched as her mother or other culinary mentors actually prepared the recipes, Irma's notes included little or no methodology. Many recipes listed only ingredients, often with no amounts. Contemporary conversion was further challenged by measurements such as "shovelful of sugar" and "butter the size of an egg" and terminology like "gem pans." Cooking times and temperatures were often vague, and recipes seldom included a test for doneness.

These challenges notwithstanding, the recipes have been rewritten to reflect an updated, if not thoroughly contemporary, format. Grocery store convenience products have, for the most part, been avoided, and labor-saving equipment, such as microwave ovens, blenders, and food processors, has been minimized or offered only as an alternative. You might say Irma's recipes have been brought into the 1960s or 1970s if not all the way into the twenty-first century.

To facilitate side-by-side comparisons between the original recipes and the updated ones, the recipes in the appendix are in the identical order as the recipes within the individual chapters. In other words, the first recipe in the appendix is Coffee, which is also the first recipe that appears in the book. To find a recipe based on its name or food category, refer to the Recipe Index.

Essen Sie gut!

Coffee

INGREDIENTS

1 egg
1/2 cup water
2/3 cup freshly ground coffee
2 quarts water

Method
Combine beaten egg (if desired, reserve shell and crumble) and
1/2 cup water; stir in ground coffee. (If desired, stir in crumbled
eggshell.) In a large pot, bring 2 quarts water to a boil, then add
egg mixture. Continue boiling gently and stirring until foam
disappears, about 4 minutes. Cover and remove from heat; allow to settle for about 7 to 10 minutes. To serve, either ladle
clear coffee off the top or strain through a cheesecloth or fine
strainer.

Yield
Makes approximately 1 1/2 quarts.

Bread Torte (*Brod Tort*)

INGREDIENTS

4 egg yolks
3/4 cup granulated sugar
1 1/2 ounces unsweetened chocolate, melted
1/2 teaspoon cinnamon
1/4 teaspoon powdered ginger
4 egg whites
1 1/2 cups day-old bread cubes
1/3 cup slivered almonds

Method
Beat egg yolks with sugar using a wire whisk or electric mixer until thick and lemon-colored. Stir in melted chocolate, cinnamon, and ginger. In a large bowl, beat egg whites using a wire whisk or electric mixer until stiff peaks form, about 1 1/2 to 2 minutes. Fold egg-yolk mixture into beaten egg whites using a wooden spoon or rubber spatula. Fold bread cubes and almonds into mixture. Pour into well-greased 9- x 9-inch baking pan. Bake at 350 degrees for 25 minutes or until top is golden brown.

Yield
Makes 6 to 8 servings.

Bread Pudding No. 1 (*Brod Pudding*)

8 slices day-old bread, crusts removed, cubed
1/4 cup water
2 tablespoons melted butter
1/2 cup granulated sugar
1/2 teaspoon cinnamon
1/4 teaspoon salt
2 eggs
1/2 teaspoon vanilla
1 teaspoon lemon juice
1/3 cup slivered almonds

Method
Soak bread cubes in water to soften; squeeze out excess water. Pour melted butter into 9- x 13-inch baking pan and spread evenly over bottom. Pat bread into pan. Combine sugar, cinnamon, and salt. Add beaten eggs, vanilla, and lemon juice; mix well. Pour over bread; sprinkle with almonds. Bake at 350 degrees for 35 to 40 minutes until puffy and golden brown.

Yield
Makes 8 to 10 servings.

Bread Pudding No. 2 (Brod Pudding)

INGREDIENTS
8 slices day-old bread, crusts removed, cubed
1/4 cup water
1 tablespoon melted butter
5 tablespoons granulated sugar
1/2 teaspoon cinnamon
1/4 teaspoon salt
1 egg

Method
Soak bread in water to soften; squeeze out excess water. Pour melted butter into 9- x 9-inch baking pan and spread evenly over bottom. Pat bread into pan. Combine sugar, cinnamon, and salt. Add beaten egg; mix well. Pour over bread. Bake at 350 degrees for 35 to 40 minutes until puffy and golden brown.

Yield
Makes 6 to 8 servings.

Jelly Roll

INGREDIENTS

3 eggs
1 cup granulated sugar
1 cup flour
1 teaspoon baking powder
1/2 cup heavy cream, whipped
Powdered sugar
1/2 cup jelly or jam

Method
Beat eggs with sugar using a wire whisk or electric mixer until thick and lemon-colored. Mix together flour and baking powder; gradually stir into egg mixture until blended. Using a wooden spoon or rubber spatula, fold whipped cream into egg and flour mixture until blended. Pour batter into 10 1/2- x 15 1/2- x 1-inch jelly roll pan lined with buttered parchment. Bake at 375 degrees for 15 minutes. Immediately run a small knife or spatula around sides to loosen cake and turn out onto a cotton towel that has been sprinkled with powdered sugar. Starting at long end, roll cake and towel together and allow cake to cool. Unroll; remove towel, spread cake with jelly or jam, and roll up. Cut into 3/4-inch slices.

Yield
Makes 20 to 24 slices.

Sponge Cake *(Spongue Cake)*

INGREDIENTS

7 egg yolks
1 cup granulated sugar
7 egg whites
7 tablespoons flour
1 1/2 teaspoons baking powder

Method
Beat egg yolks with sugar using a wire whisk or electric mixer until thick and lemon-colored. Mix together flour and baking powder; gradually stir into egg mixture until blended. In a large bowl, beat egg whites using a wire whisk or electric mixer until stiff peaks form, about 1 1/2 to 2 minutes. Fold the egg yolk mixture into the beaten egg whites until blended, using a wooden spoon or rubber spatula. Pour batter into an ungreased 9- x 13-inch baking pan. Bake at 350 degrees for 25 to 30 minutes until top springs back.

Yield
Makes 1 9- x 13-inch cake.

Cream Sponge Cake

INGREDIENTS

3 eggs
1 cup powdered sugar
1 cup flour
1 teaspoon baking powder
1/2 cup heavy cream, whipped

Method
Beat egg yolks with powdered sugar using a wire whisk or electric mixer until thick and lemon-colored. Mix together flour and baking powder; gradually stir into egg mixture until blended. Fold whipped cream into egg and flour mixture until blended using a wooden spoon or rubber spatula. Pour batter into greased and floured 9- x 13-inch baking pan. Bake at 350 degrees for 25 minutes or until top is lightly browned.

Yield
Makes 1 9- x 13-inch cake.

Maple Sugar Cake

1 cup butter, softened
2 cups granulated sugar
4 eggs
3 cups flour
1 teaspoon baking powder
1 cup milk

Maple Sugar Filling:
1 cup real maple syrup
5 egg whites
1/2 teaspoon cream of tartar

Method
Cream butter and sugar until light and fluffy. Add eggs and continue beating until blended. Sift together flour and baking powder. Add flour mixture to creamed mixture alternately with milk, beating well after each addition. Pour batter into 2 greased and floured 8- or 9-inch round cake pans. Bake at 350 degrees for 30 minutes or until wooden pick inserted in center comes out clean. Cool 10 minutes. Remove from pans. Fill and frost with Maple Sugar Filling.

Maple Sugar Filling: Bring maple syrup to boil in a heavy 3-quart saucepan and cook, without stirring, to 238 to 240 degrees or until a soft ball can be formed when small amount is dropped into cold water, about 5 minutes. Cool slightly. While syrup is cooling, beat egg whites using a wire whisk or electric mixer until stiff peaks begin to form, about 1 1/2 to 2 minutes. Add cream of tartar and continue to beat egg whites while slowly pouring syrup in a thin stream. Continue beating to spreading consistency.

Yield
Makes 1 8- or 9-inch layer cake.

Caramel Cake

INGREDIENTS

1/2 cup butter, softened
2 cups granulated sugar
3 eggs
2 teaspoons grated lemon rind
1 tablespoon lemon juice
2 cups flour
2 teaspoons baking powder

Caramel Icing
2 cups dark brown sugar
1/2 cup heavy cream
2 tablespoons butter

Method
Cream together butter and sugar until light and fluffy. Add eggs, lemon rind, and lemon juice, beating until blended. Sift together flour and baking powder. Add flour mixture to creamed mixture, beating until well blended. Spread batter into greased and floured 9- x 13-inch baking pan. Bake at 350 degrees for 30 minutes or until wooden pick inserted in center comes out clean. Cool 10 minutes. Pour Caramel Icing over warm cake.

Caramel Icing: Combine brown sugar, cream, and butter in heavy 3-quart saucepan. Bring to a boil, and cook, without stirring, to 238 to 240 degrees or until soft ball can be formed when small amount of mixture is dropped into cold water, about 5 minutes. Remove from heat; cool slightly and pour over Caramel Cake.

Yield
Makes 1 9- x 13-inch cake.

Chocolate Cake

INGREDIENTS

1/2 cup butter, softened
1 1/2 cups granulated sugar
4 egg yolks
1 teaspoon vanilla
2 ounces unsweetened chocolate
5 tablespoons water
1/2 cup milk
1 3/4 cups flour
1 1/2 teaspoons baking powder
4 egg whites

Method
Cream butter and sugar until light and fluffy. Add egg yolks and vanilla and continue beating until blended. Combine chocolate and water in small saucepan and heat just until chocolate melts. Stir melted chocolate mixture into creamed mixture until blended. Sift together flour and baking powder. Add flour mixture and milk to creamed mixture, mixing until well blended. Beat egg whites using a wire whisk or electric mixer until stiff peaks form, about 1 1/2 to 2 minutes. Fold into batter until blended using wooden spoon or rubber spatula. Pour batter into 2 greased and floured 8- or 9-inch round cake pans. Bake at 350 degrees for 30 minutes or until wooden pick inserted in center comes out clean. Cool 10 minutes. Remove from pans.

Yield
Makes 2 8- or 9-inch cake layers.

Chocolate Frosting

INGREDIENTS

4 egg whites
1 cup powdered sugar, sifted
1 teaspoon vanilla
1/2 teaspoon cream of tartar
1 1/2 ounces unsweetened chocolate, melted

Method
Beat egg whites using a wire whisk or electric mixer until very
soft peaks form, about 1 1/2 minutes. Continue beating while
gradually adding sifted powdered sugar. Add vanilla and cream
of tartar, beating until stiff peaks form and frosting is glossy.
Fold in melted chocolate until thoroughly blended using a
wooden spoon or rubber spatula.

Yield
Makes enough to frost 1 single-layer cake or 1 angel food cake.

Cup Cake No. 1

1 cup butter, softened
1 1/4 cups granulated sugar
4 egg yolks
3 cups sifted flour
2 teaspoons baking powder
1 cup milk
4 egg whites

Method
Cream together butter and sugar until light and fluffy. Add egg yolks and continue beating until fluffy. Sift together flour and baking powder. Add flour mixture to creamed mixture alternately with milk, beating well after each addition. Beat egg whites using a wire whisk or electric mixer until stiff peaks form, about 1 1/2 to 2 minutes. Fold egg whites into batter using a wooden spoon or rubber spatula. Grease muffin pans or line with paper muffin cups; fill each cup half full. Bake at 375 degrees for 20 to 25 minutes until golden brown.

Yield
Makes 24 to 30 cupcakes.

Cup Cake No. 2

INGREDIENTS

1/4 cup butter, softened
1 cup granulated sugar
5 eggs
3 cups sifted flour
2 1/2 teaspoons baking powder
1 cup milk

Method
Beat together butter, sugar, and eggs until light and fluffy. Sift to-gether flour and baking powder. Add flour mixture to creamed mixture alternately with milk, beating well after each addition. Grease muffin pans or line with paper muffin cups; fill each cup half full. Bake at 375 degrees for 20 to 25 minutes until golden brown.

Yield
Makes 18 to 20 cupcakes.

Muffins

INGREDIENTS

2 cups sifted flour
1/2 cup granulated sugar
1 1/2 teaspoons baking powder
2 eggs
1 cup milk
1 tablespoon melted butter

Method
Stir together flour, sugar, and baking powder. Combine eggs, milk, and melted butter. Add egg mixture to flour mixture; mix just until blended. Grease muffin pans or line with paper muffin cups; fill each cup two-thirds full. Bake at 400 degrees for 20 to 25 minutes until lightly browned.

Yield
Makes 18 muffins.

Johnnycake (*Johnny Cake*)

3 cups yellow cornmeal
1 1/2 cups flour
1 tablespoon granulated sugar
3 teaspoons baking powder
3 eggs
2 cups milk
1 tablespoon melted butter

Method
Stir together cornmeal, flour, sugar, and baking powder. Combine eggs, milk, and melted butter. Add egg mixture to flour mixture; mix just until blended. For each pancake, drop about 1/4 cup batter onto hot, lightly greased griddle. Cook until bubbles appear on surface and begin to burst. Flip with pancake turner and continue cooking until underside is cooked and lightly browned. Keep warm until ready to serve. Batter may also be poured into a well-greased and preheated 10-inch cast iron skillet and baked at 350 degrees for 20 to 25 minutes or until top is slightly browned and springs back. To serve, cut into 8 wedges.

Yield
Makes about 20 3 1/2-inch pancakes, or 8 servings.

Excellent Whole-Wheat Bread

INGREDIENTS

4 1/2 teaspoons active dry yeast (2 1/4-ounce
  envelopes)
1/4 cup warm water
2 cups boiling water
2 cups milk
1 teaspoon salt
8 to 10 cups whole-wheat flour (for a lighter bread, use
  half whole-wheat flour and half white flour)

Method
Soften yeast in warm water. In a large bowl, pour boiling water
into milk and cool to lukewarm. Add softened yeast and salt.
Stir in about 6 cups flour to make a thick, sticky batter. Cover
and let stand in a warm place about 3 hours until doubled in
bulk. Stir in enough flour to make a stiff dough. Turn out on
floured board and knead, sprinkling with flour if necessary, until dough is smooth and no longer sticky. Continue kneading
until thumbprint remains when thumb is pressed into dough.
Shape dough into 4 loaves. Place loaves in greased baking pans
or on greased baking sheets. Cover and let rise in warm place
about 1 hour. Bake at 375 degrees for 35 to 45 minutes until
crusts are lightly browned.

Yield
Makes 4 loaves.

Orange Marmalade *(Orange Marmelade)*

INGREDIENTS

8 oranges
3 lemons
3 1/2 cups water
1 to 1 1/2 pounds granulated sugar

Method

Remove the zest from oranges and lemons and cut into thin slivers. Discard pith and seeds; finely chop fruit pulp. Combine pulp, zest, and water in a large, heavy Dutch oven or stockpot; simmer, uncovered, for 10 minutes. Remove from heat, cover, and store in a cool place overnight. Measure pulp mixture. Return pulp to pan and add 1 1/2 cups sugar for every 1 cup of pulp mixture. Slowly heat, uncovered to boiling, stirring until sugar dissolves. Boil slowly, stirring occasionally, 30 to 40 minutes until candy thermometer reaches 218 to 220 degrees. Skim off any froth. Fill 10 6-ounce sterilized jelly jars to within 1/8 inch of tops. If desired, stir marmalade in jars to distribute zest. Seal jars with paraffin.

Yield

Makes enough to fill 10 6-ounce jelly jars.

French Potatoes

INGREDIENTS
Baking potatoes
Butter or oil
Salt and pepper (optional)

Method
Wash potatoes (and peel, if desired). Cut into strips 1/4- to 1/2-inch thick. Pat completely dry with paper towels. Heat about 1/4 inch melted butter or oil in a heavy skillet. Add potatoes. Cook slowly, one layer at a time, turning to brown, until center is tender, about 10 minutes. Add more butter or oil during cooking, if needed. Drain on paper towels. Season to taste.

Green Peas

INGREDIENTS

2 tablespoons melted butter
2 tablespoons flour
1 cup water or beef or chicken broth
2 cups cooked peas or 1 16-ounce can peas, drained
2 tablespoons chopped fresh parsley
Salt
Black pepper

Method
Combine melted butter and flour in saucepan. Add water or broth and bring to a boil, cooking and stirring until thickened. Stir in peas and parsley. Season to taste.

Yield
Makes 4 to 6 servings.

Breast of Veal with Dressing

INGREDIENTS

2 slices bacon, chopped
1 medium onion, chopped
4 cups soft bread crumbs
2 tablespoons chopped fresh parsley
Salt
Black pepper
1 egg, beaten
1 3-pound veal breast with pocket cut for stuffing
4 carrots, peeled and cut into 2-inch pieces
1 bay leaf
2 cups beef broth

Method

Cook bacon in a Dutch oven or roasting pan until limp; add onion and continue cooking until bacon is crisp and onion is tender; drain, reserving 1 tablespoon drippings. Toss together bread crumbs and parsley; season to taste with salt and pepper. Combine bread crumb mixture with beaten egg; mix well. Stuff pocket of veal with bread and egg dressing; close and secure with skewers or heavy thread. Season surface of veal with salt and pepper; brown on all sides in reserved bacon drippings in Dutch oven. Add cooked bacon and onion, carrots, and bay leaf. Bake, covered, at 350 degrees, basting occasionally with beef broth, for 2 hours or until meat is tender. Place veal and vegetables on serving platter. Add remaining broth to pan and bring to boil to deglaze pan and reduce broth; thicken with flour, if desired. Pour broth over veal.

Yield
Makes 4 to 6 servings.

Pot Roast

INGREDIENTS

1 2-pound chuck roast or pot roast
Flour
2 stalks celery, cut into 2-inch pieces
6 carrots, peeled and cut into 2-inch pieces
1 medium onion, coarsely chopped
Salt
Black pepper

Method
Trim meat and dredge with flour; brown on all sides in small amount of fat in a Dutch oven or deep heavy skillet. Add about 1/2 cup water; bring to a boil. Reduce heat and simmer, covered, 1 1/2 hours, adding water if needed to prevent sticking. Add vegetables; cover and continue simmering 1 to 2 hours until meat is tender. Thicken broth with flour, if desired. Season to taste.

Yield
Makes 4 to 6 servings.

Baked Sweetbreads

INGREDIENTS
3/4 pound sweetbreads, washed, cleaned
1 egg, beaten
3/4 cup dry bread crumbs
Salt
Black pepper
2 tablespoons melted butter

Method
Soak sweetbreads in warm water for about 1 hour; drain. Poach in boiling water for about 10 minutes; drain and pat dry. Dip sweetbreads into beaten egg, then into bread crumbs; repeat. Place in greased baking dish; season with salt and pepper. Drizzle with melted butter. Bake at 325 degrees for 20 to 30 minutes until very lightly browned.

Yield
Makes 2 servings.

Cream Sauce

INGREDIENTS
2 tablespoons butter
2 tablespoons flour
1 cup milk
1 egg yolk (optional)

Method
In medium saucepan, melt butter over medium heat; stir in flour until smooth and blended. Gradually add milk, stirring with a wire whisk or wooden spoon. Cook over medium heat just until boiling, stirring constantly until mixture thickens. If desired, stir small amount of hot mixture into egg yolk. Return egg mixture to saucepan and continue cooking, stirring constantly, for an additional 2 minutes. Season with salt and pepper, if desired.

Yield
Makes 1 cup.

Creamed Celery

INGREDIENTS
1 bunch celery
1 cup Cream Sauce (p. 124)
Salt

Method
Wash stalks and cut into 1-inch pieces, discarding tops. Place celery in saucepan and cover with water. Simmer 1 hour or until celery is tender; drain. Combine cooked celery and Cream Sauce. Season to taste.

Yield
Makes 4 to 6 servings.

Celery Stew

INGREDIENTS

1 bunch celery
1 cup beef, chicken, or vegetable stock
1 tablespoon melted butter
1 tablespoon flour
Salt

Method

Wash stalks and cut into 1-inch pieces, discarding tops and bottoms. Place celery in saucepan with stock. Simmer 30 minutes or until celery is tender. Drain, reserving liquid. Combine melted butter and flour in saucepan; stir in reserved liquid. Cook over medium heat, stirring constantly, until thickened. Stir in celery. Season to taste.

Yield

Makes 4 to 6 servings.

Celery au Jus

INGREDIENTS

1 bunch celery
3 cups beef or chicken broth
2 tablespoons butter
2 tablespoons flour
1/8 teaspoon black pepper

Method
Wash stalks and cut into 6-inch pieces, discarding tops and bottoms. Simmer celery in broth 5 minutes. Drain, reserving 2 cups broth. Melt butter in saucepan and add flour. Cook slowly over low heat, stirring constantly until flour browns, about 5 minutes. Add reserved broth; cook over medium heat, stirring constantly until thickened. Add celery and pepper; cover and simmer 25 minutes or until celery is tender, stirring occasionally.

Yield
Makes 4 to 6 servings.

Spinach *(Spinnage)*

INGREDIENTS

2 pounds fresh spinach
1/4 cup chopped onion
2 tablespoons butter
1 cup beef or chicken broth
Salt
Black pepper

Method
Rinse spinach and remove any large, coarse stems; shake off excess water. Place spinach in a large skillet; cover and cook over medium-high heat until wilted and tender, about 4 to 5 minutes. Drain, if needed, and chop. In a saucepan, cook onion in butter until tender; stir in flour. Add water or broth and bring to a boil, cooking and stirring until thickened. Stir in spinach. Season to taste.

Yield
Makes 4 to 6 servings.

Rice Soup

1 1-pound chuck roast or pot roast
3 quarts water
4 stalks celery, cut into 1/4-inch pieces
4 medium tomatoes, coarsely chopped
6 carrots, peeled and cut into 1/4-inch pieces
1 medium onion, coarsely chopped
1/2 cup long-grain white rice, cooked
Salt
Black pepper

Method
Trim meat and brown on both sides in small amount of fat in a Dutch oven or stockpot. Add 4 cups water; cover and simmer until meat is tender and falls from bone, about 1 1/2 to 2 hours. Remove meat and cut into small pieces. Return meat to water in pot; add remaining 2 quarts water and vegetables. Bring to boil and skim off froth, if necessary. Reduce heat and continue simmering until vegetables are tender, about 45 minutes to 1 hour. Stir in cooked rice. Thicken with flour, if desired. Season to taste.

Yield
Makes 8 to 10 servings.

Green Kern Soup

INGREDIENTS
1 cup freekeh (dried green wheat)
10 cups beef, chicken, or vegetable stock
Salt
Black pepper

Method
Wash and sort freekeh, removing any hulls or discolored kernels. Soak in 4 cups water for 1/2 hour; drain and rinse. Combine freekeh and stock in large pot. Bring to a boil; reduce heat and simmer for 2 hours or until freekeh is tender. Season to taste.

Yield
Makes 8 to 10 servings.

Note
Freekeh is available at Middle Eastern specialty food stores or health food stores.

Peas Soup

16 ounces dried split green peas
8 cups water
1 teaspoon salt
1 teaspoon lemon juice
1 teaspoon vinegar
1 tablespoon granulated sugar
3 tablespoons flour
Salt
Black pepper

Method
Wash and sort peas, discarding any discolored peas. Combine peas and water in large pot. Bring to a boil; reduce heat and simmer 1 1/2 hours or until peas are soft. Skim off any froth. Put mixture through a food mill or process in a blender until smooth. Return mixture to pot and stir in salt, lemon juice, vinegar, and sugar; bring to boil. Combine flour with small amount of cold water to make a thick liquid. Pour flour mixture into soup and continue cooking and stirring until thickened. Season to taste.

Yield
Makes 8 servings.

Vegetable Soup

INGREDIENTS

1 pound chuck roast or pot roast
3 quarts water
4 stalks celery, cut into 1/4-inch pieces
4 medium tomatoes, coarsely chopped
6 carrots, peeled and cut into 1/4-inch pieces
1 medium onion, coarsely chopped
2 medium potatoes, peeled and chopped
Salt
Black pepper

Method
Trim meat and brown on both sides in small amount of fat in a Dutch oven or stockpot. Add 4 cups water; cover and simmer until meat is tender and falls from bone. Remove meat and cut into small pieces. Return meat to water in pot; add remaining water and vegetables. Bring to boil and skim off froth, if necessary. Reduce heat and continue simmering until vegetables are tender, about 45 minutes to 1 hour. Thicken with flour, if desired. Season to taste.

Yield
Makes 8 to 10 servings.

Fish

INGREDIENTS

4 whole fish (about 4 pounds)
Salt
2 celery stalks, cut into 1/2-inch pieces
1 medium onion, chopped
2 carrots, peeled, cut into 1/2-inch pieces
4 cups water

Method
Fillet fish, reserving heads and tails. Salt fish fillets and allow to stand about 30 minutes; rinse off salt. Place fish heads and tails in bottom of a Dutch oven or stockpot. Add fish fillets, celery, onion, carrots, and water. Bring to a boil and simmer 30 to 45 minutes or until fish is tender. Discard fish heads and tails. Serve vegetables with fish.

Yield
Makes 6 to 8 servings.

Sour Fish

INGREDIENTS
4 whole fish (about 4 pounds)
Salt
4 cups water
1/2 cup cider vinegar
1/2 cup brown sugar
1/4 cup raisins
2 medium onions, sliced
1/2 lemon
6 ginger snaps, crumbled

Method
Fillet fish, reserving heads and tails. Salt fish fillets and allow to stand about 30 minutes; rinse off salt. In a Dutch oven or stockpot combine fish heads and tails, water, vinegar, sugar, raisins, onions, and lemon. Simmer about 30 minutes to develop flavor. Remove fish heads and tails, and discard. Add fish fillets to stock and simmer about 20 minutes until fillets are tender. Arrange fish, onions, and raisins on serving platter. Discard lemon; strain stock, if needed. Add ginger snaps to stock and cook until thickened. Pour over fish. May be served warm or chilled.

Yield
Makes 6 to 8 servings.

Sharp Fish No. 1

INGREDIENTS

1 small onion, finely chopped
1 clove garlic, chopped
1 tablespoon butter
1/4 teaspoon ground ginger
1/2 teaspoon salt
1/2 teaspoon black pepper
1 tablespoon lemon juice
1 pound fish fillets
2 cups water
2 teaspoons cornstarch
1 egg yolk
2 tablespoons chopped fresh parsley
Pickled or crystallized ginger for garnish (optional)

Method

Cook onion and garlic in butter in a Dutch oven or deep skillet until onion is tender; add ginger, salt, pepper, lemon juice, fish fillets, and water. Bring to a boil and simmer just until fish is tender, about 6 to 10 minutes. Place fish on serving platter. Reserve 1 cup cooking liquid. Combine cornstarch and about 1 tablespoon cold water; stir into reserved cooking liquid in pan. Bring to a boil and cook, stirring constantly until thickened. Stir a small amount of the hot mixture into egg yolk. Return egg mixture to saucepan and continue cooking, stirring constantly an additional 2 minutes. Stir in parsley. Serve over fish. Garnish with pickled or crystallized ginger, if desired.

Yield

Makes 2 servings.

Sharp Fish No. 2

INGREDIENTS

1 small onion, finely chopped
1 clove garlic, chopped
1 tablespoon butter
2 tablespoons chopped fresh parsley
1/4 teaspoon ground ginger
1/2 teaspoon salt
1/2 teaspoon black pepper
1 tablespoon lemon juice
1 pound fish fillets
2 cups water
Melted butter

Method
Cook onion and garlic in 1 tablespoon butter in a Dutch oven or deep skillet until onion is tender; add parsley, ginger, salt, pepper, lemon juice, fish fillets, and water. Bring to a boil and simmer just until fish is tender, about 6 to 10 minutes. Place fish on serving platter and drizzle with melted butter.

Yield
Makes 2 servings.

Sauce for Fish *(Sös)*

INGREDIENTS

1 teaspoon cornstarch
1/2 teaspoon granulated sugar
1 tablespoon cold water
1 cup fish stock
3 egg yolks, beaten
1 teaspoon spicy brown mustard
Juice of 1 lemon
2 teaspoons chopped parsley

Method
Combine cornstarch and sugar; stir in about 1 tablespoon cold water. In a saucepan, combine cornstarch mixture and fish stock; bring to a boil and cook, stirring constantly until thickened. Stir a small amount of the hot mixture into egg yolks. Return egg mixture to saucepan and continue cooking, stirring constantly, an additional 2 minutes. Stir in mustard, lemon juice, and parsley. Chill. Serve with fish.

Yield
Makes approximately 1 cup.

Baked Fish

INGREDIENTS
1 cup fresh bread crumbs
2 teaspoons finely chopped onion
2 teaspoons chopped parsley
Salt
Black pepper
Whole fish (about 5 pounds), cleaned and scaled
2 slices bacon

Tomato Sauce
1 29-ounce can whole tomatoes
1 small onion, chopped
2 tablespoons melted butter
2 tablespoons flour
8 whole cloves

Method
Combine bread crumbs, onion, parsley, 1/4 teaspoon salt, and 1/4 teaspoon pepper. Salt and pepper cavity of fish; stuff with bread crumb mixture. Secure with skewers or wooden picks. Place stuffed fish on baking pan lined with greased aluminum foil. Score surface of fish and cover with bacon slices. Bake at 325 degrees for 30 to 40 minutes or until fish flakes easily with a fork.

Tomato Sauce: Drain and chop tomatoes, reserving liquid. Add enough water to reserved liquid to make 1 cup. In medium saucepan, sauté onion in melted butter until tender; add flour. Stir in reserved liquid, tomatoes, and cloves. Cook over medium heat, stirring constantly, until thickened; remove cloves. Serve over fish.

Yield
Makes 8 to 10 servings.

Scalloped Fish

INGREDIENTS
3 cups cooked, flaked fish
1 1/2 cups fresh bread crumbs
3 tablespoons melted butter
1 cup milk
2 eggs, beaten

Method
In a well-greased 1 1/2-quart baking dish, layer 1 cup flaked fish and 1/2 cup bread crumbs; drizzle with 1 tablespoon melted butter. Repeat layers. Mix milk and eggs together; pour over fish. Bake at 350 degrees for 35 minutes or until golden brown. Season to taste.

Yield
Makes 6 to 8 servings.

Deviled Oysters

INGREDIENTS

1/4 cup butter
1/4 cup flour
2/3 cup milk
1 egg yolk
1 pint oysters, washed, drained, chopped
1/4 teaspoon salt
Dash of cayenne
2 teaspoons lemon juice
2 teaspoons chopped parsley
1 cup saltine cracker crumbs
Melted butter

Method

In medium saucepan, melt butter and add flour; stir in milk. Cook over medium heat, stirring constantly, until thickened. Stir a small amount of the hot mixture into egg yolk. Return egg mixture to saucepan. Stir in oysters, salt, cayenne, lemon juice, and parsley. Drop spoonfuls of oyster mixture into 8 greased scallop shells or shallow individual ramekins; sprinkle with cracker crumbs; drizzle with melted butter. Place on baking sheet. Bake at 450 degrees for 15 minutes or until cracker crumbs are golden brown.

Yield

Makes 8 first-course servings.

Oysters in Baskets

INGREDIENTS
10 large-size shredded wheat biscuits
Salt
Black pepper
1/2 cup butter
1 pint fresh oysters

Method
Cut oblong section from top of each shredded wheat biscuit and remove loose shreds to form 1/2-inch shell; crumble and reserve removed shredded wheat covers. Place shells on baking sheet. Place 1/2 teaspoon butter in each shell; sprinkle with salt and pepper. Drain oysters, reserving liquid. Arrange oysters in shells; sprinkle with salt and pepper. Drizzle about 2 teaspoons reserved oyster liquid over each shell. Sprinkle reserved shredded wheat crumbs over shells. Melt remaining butter; drizzle butter over oyster baskets. Bake at 350 degrees for 15 to 20 minutes or until slightly browned. Serve with Cream Sauce (p. 124), substituting remaining oyster liquid for part of the milk, if desired.

Yield
Makes 10 first-course servings or 5 main-course servings.

Oysters with Celery

INGREDIENTS
2 cups chopped celery
2 tablespoons butter
1/4 cup cream
1 teaspoon salt
1/4 teaspoon cayenne pepper
1 teaspoon cornstarch
1 tablespoon cold water
12 fresh oysters, drained
2 slices buttered toast

Method
Sauté celery in butter until tender. Add cream, salt, and cayenne. Mix together cornstarch and cold water; stir into celery mixture. Cook, stirring constantly until thickened. Add oysters; continue cooking just until oysters begin to ruffle. To serve, pour over buttered toast.

Yield
Makes 2 servings.

Deviled Meat

1 tablespoon butter
2/3 cup coarse bread crumbs
1/2 teaspoon dry mustard
Salt
Pepper
2 cups finely chopped cooked beef
2 hard-cooked egg yolks, sieved
4 to 6 slices buttered toast

Method
Melt butter in skillet; add bread crumbs and cook, stirring occasionally, until bread crumbs are brown and crisp. Add dry mustard; salt and pepper to taste. Stir in cooked beef and heat thoroughly, stirring occasionally. Stir in sieved egg yolks. Serve over hot buttered toast.

Yield
Makes 4 to 6 servings.

Surprise Sausages

Cooked sausages
Mashed potatoes
Beaten Egg
Dry Bread crumbs
Melted butter

Method
Cut sausages into 1-inch pieces; remove skin or casing, if desired. Pat dry. Shape about 2 tablespoons of mashed potatoes around each sausage piece. Dip in beaten egg; roll in bread crumbs. Chill at least 1 hour. Deep fry until golden brown or place on a baking sheet, drizzle with melted butter, and bake at 400 degrees for 15 to 20 minutes or until browned.

Omelet

INGREDIENTS
3 eggs
1 teaspoon water
Pinch of salt
1 tablespoon butter

Method
Beat together eggs, water, and salt until blended but not frothy.
Heat a skillet or omelet pan and add butter. Cook butter until
it sizzles and just begins to brown; tilt pan to completely grease
bottom and sides. Add egg mixture, tilting pan to distribute
evenly. Continue cooking over medium-high heat. As edges
cook, lift slightly with spatula to allow uncooked portion to
flow underneath. Run spatula around edge to prevent sticking.
When surface is set but not dry, fold in half and slide to serving
plate.

Yield
Makes 1 omelet.

Beauregard Eggs

5 hard-cooked eggs
1 tablespoon butter
1 tablespoon flour
1 cup milk
Salt
Pepper
4 slices buttered toast

Method
Cut eggs in half; remove yolks. Sieve whites and yolks separately. In medium saucepan, melt butter and add flour; stir in milk. Cook over medium heat, stirring constantly, until thickened. Stir in egg whites; season to taste. Arrange toast on warm, oven-proof platter; pour egg mixture over toast. Sprinkle with sieved egg yolks. Place under broiler about 1 minute, or just long enough to reheat.

Yield
Makes 4 servings.

Stuffed Eggs

2 eggs, beaten
1 tablespoon cream
2 tablespoons olive oil
2 teaspoons vinegar
1 teaspoon dry mustard
1/2 teaspoon salt
1/2 teaspoon black pepper
10 hard-cooked eggs

Method
In top of a double boiler, combine beaten eggs, cream, oil, and vinegar. Mix together mustard, salt, and pepper; add to egg mixture. Cook in double boiler over boiling water, stirring constantly with a wire whisk, until thickened. Cool. Cut eggs in half; remove and mash yolks. Add cooked mixture to yolks; mix well. Refill whites. Refrigerate until ready to serve.

Yield
Makes 20 egg halves.

Egg Salad

8 hard-cooked eggs
Softened butter
1/2 teaspoon granulated sugar
1/4 teaspoon celery seed
Salt
Pepper
1/2 cup finely chopped cooked chicken breast
8 slices white bread, crusts removed

Method
Cut eggs in half; remove and mash yolks. Add enough butter to yolks for a spreadable consistency, about 2 tablespoons. Add sugar and celery seed and season to taste. Add chicken; stir until blended. Refill whites. Make sandwiches with bread and butter; cut into triangles. Serve butter sandwiches with eggs.

Yield
Makes 6 to 8 servings.

Celery for Garnish

Celery stalks
Ice water

Method
Wash celery stalks and cut into 2-inch pieces, discarding tops and bottoms. With a sharp knife, split each piece about 6 times to within 1/2 inch of the bottom. Soak in bowl of ice water in refrigerator for several hours or overnight. Celery will curl.

Celery Salad

2 cups chopped celery
12 pitted ripe olives, chopped
1/2 cup chopped walnuts
1 teaspoon salt
Pinch of cayenne pepper
1/2 teaspoon lemon juice
Mayonnaise (p. 152)

Method
Combine celery, olives, walnuts, salt, cayenne, and lemon juice; mix lightly. Refrigerate until ready to serve. Serve topped with a dollop of mayonnaise.

Yield
Makes 4 to 6 servings.

Cherry Salad

INGREDIENTS
Sweet cherries
Whole blanched hazelnuts
Lettuce
Mayonnaise (p. 152)

Method
Pit and halve cherries. Place a hazelnut in center of each cherry half. Arrange cherries on lettuce on serving platter. Serve with mayonnaise.

Mayonnaise *(Mayonnaissee)*

INGREDIENTS

1 teaspoon cornstarch
1 teaspoon dry mustard
1/4 cup water
2 tablespoons white wine vinegar
3 egg yolks
2 tablespoons oil

Method
Combine cornstarch and dry mustard; stir in water until blended. In the top of a double boiler, beat egg yolks and vinegar with a wire whisk. Stir in cornstarch mixture. Cook over boiling water until thickened. Slowly add oil in a thin stream continuing to beat vigorously until blended. Stir to cool. Store in refrigerator.

Yield
Makes approximately 1/2 cup.

Boiled Salad Dressing

INGREDIENTS

2 tablespoons granulated sugar
1 teaspoon cornstarch
1 teaspoon dry mustard
1 teaspoon salt
1/4 teaspoon cayenne pepper
1/4 cup cold milk
6 egg yolks
3/4 cup milk
1/4 cup white wine vinegar
2 tablespoons butter
1/2 cup heavy cream, whipped

Method
Combine sugar, cornstarch, mustard, salt, and cayenne; stir in 1/4 cup milk until blended. In top of a double boiler, combine egg yolks, 3/4 cup milk, and vinegar. Add butter; heat over boiling water until butter melts. Stir in cornstarch mixture. Cook over boiling water, stirring constantly with a wire whisk, until thickened. Stir to cool. Fold into whipped cream. Store in refrigerator.

Yield
Makes approximately 3 cups.

Mayonnaise (1910)

INGREDIENTS

2 eggs, beaten
1/4 cup white wine vinegar
2 tablespoons oil
1 teaspoon granulated sugar
1/2 teaspoon dry mustard
1/4 teaspoon paprika
1/2 teaspoon salt
1/4 teaspoon cayenne pepper
1/2 cup heavy cream, whipped

Method
Combine eggs, vinegar, and oil in top of a double boiler. Cook over boiling water, stirring constantly with a wire whisk, until thickened. Mix together sugar, mustard, paprika, salt, and cayenne; stir into egg mixture. Stir to cool. Fold into whipped cream. Chill. Store in refrigerator.

Yield
Makes 1 1/2 cups.

Peanut Sandwiches

INGREDIENTS
Thin white bread slices, crusts removed
Mayonnaise (p. 152)
Spanish peanuts

Method
Spread bread lightly with mayonnaise; sprinkle with peanuts.
Cut each slice into 4 triangles.

Raisin Sandwiches

INGREDIENTS

Thin white bread slices, crusts removed
Softened butter
Raisins
Brandy or sweet sherry

Method
Lightly spread bread with butter. Arrange raisins closely together over butter. Lightly drizzle with brandy or sherry. Cut
each slice into 4 triangles.

Nasturtium Sandwiches

INGREDIENTS

Thin white bread slices, crusts removed
Softened butter
Fresh nasturtium flowers, washed, chilled
Salt
Black pepper

Method
Lightly spread bread with butter. Arrange nasturtiums on butter.
Sprinkle lightly with salt and pepper. Top with second slice of
bread spread with butter. Cut each sandwich into 4 triangles.

Kisses

INGREDIENTS

4 egg whites
1 cup powdered sugar, sifted
1/2 teaspoon cream of tartar
1/2 teaspoon vanilla

Method
Beat egg whites with a wire whisk or electric mixer until soft peaks form. Continue beating, while gradually adding sifted powdered sugar. Add cream of tartar and vanilla, beating until stiff peaks form and mixture is glossy. Drop by teaspoonfuls onto parchment-lined baking sheet. Bake at 225 degrees for 1 hour or until lightly browned. Turn off oven and allow cookies to dry overnight.

Yield
Makes 3 1/2 to 4 dozen kisses.

Chilled Orange Custard

6 oranges, juiced
1/2 cup granulated sugar
6 egg yolks
2 cups half and half or heavy cream

Method
Combine juice from oranges and sugar; heat in saucepan until sugar dissolves. Stir a small amount of the hot mixture into egg yolks. Return egg mixture to saucepan, add half and half or cream, and continue cooking over medium heat, stirring constantly, until mixture thickens. Stir to cool slightly. Pour into 4 6-ounce custard cups or dessert dishes. Chill thoroughly, at least 4 hours.

Yield
Makes 4 servings.

Pie Crust

2 cups flour
2 tablespoons sugar
1 teaspoon salt
2/3 cup butter
1 egg yolk
1/4 cup cold water

Method
Combine flour, sugar, and salt; cut in butter with a pastry blender or 2 kitchen knives until pieces are the size of small peas. Mix together egg yolk and water; gently mix into flour mixture just enough for dough to form a ball. Add additional water if needed. Chill until ready to use.

Yield
Makes enough for a 2-crust pie.

Plain Pastry

INGREDIENTS

2 cups flour
1/2 teaspoon baking powder
1/2 teaspoon salt
3/4 cup very cold butter, divided
6 to 8 tablespoons cold water

Method
Combine flour, baking powder, and salt. Cut in half of the butter (about 6 tablespoons) with a pastry blender or 2 kitchen knives until pieces are the size of small peas. Lightly mix in just enough cold water for dough to form a ball. Turn onto lightly floured board and pat or roll into oblong shape about 6 by 8 inches. Spread with 1 tablespoon of remaining butter and lightly dust with flour. Fold one side to the middle, and then fold over the other side. Fold in half to square. Roll or pat into oblong shape and repeat until all butter is used. Dough may be chilled for later use.

Yield
Makes enough for 2 9-inch tart shells or 24 to 30 miniature tart shells.

Note
See Pie Crust (p. 160) for a classic pie dough.

Blackberry Cream

INGREDIENTS

1 pint fresh blackberries
Granulated sugar
Dried coarse bread crumbs
2 egg whites
2 tablespoons granulated sugar
1 cup heavy cream, whipped
Ladyfingers

Method
Press berries through a sieve or colander to extract juice. Discard pulp and seeds. For each cup of fruit juice, add 1/2 cup sugar; bring to boil and cook until sugar is melted. Stir in 1/4 cup bread crumbs for each 1/2 cup sugar. Return to boil, then immediately remove from heat. Cool slightly; pour into serving bowl or individual dessert dishes. Chill. Beat egg whites until soft peaks form. Gradually add sugar, beating until stiff peaks form. Fold in whipped cream. To serve, spoon whipped cream mixture over berry mixture. Serve with ladyfingers.

Yield
Makes 4 servings.

Cream Raspberry Tart

INGREDIENTS

Pie Crust (p. 160)
4 cups fresh raspberries
3/4 cup plus 1 tablespoon granulated sugar, divided
1 tablespoon plus 1/2 teaspoon cornstarch, divided
1 cup heavy cream
2 egg whites, beaten to stiff peaks

Method
Roll out half of pie crust and fit into pie plate or tart pan; trim edge. Fill pastry with raspberries. Combine 3/4 cup sugar and 1 tablespoon cornstarch; sprinkle over berries. Roll out remaining crust about 1/2 inch larger than top or pan. Gently lay top crust over berries. Cut several small slits in crust to vent steam. Bake at 400 degrees for 40 to 45 minutes or until golden brown. Cool completely. Combine 1 tablespoon sugar and 1/2 teaspoon cornstarch; stir in 1 tablespoon cream. Heat remaining cream just to boiling; slowly add cornstarch mixture, stirring constantly. Continue simmering, stirring constantly, until thickened. Remove from heat; fold in beaten egg whites. Stir to cool. Carefully remove top crust. Spoon cream and egg white mixture over berries; replace crust. Serve immediately.

Yield
Makes 1 large tart.

Note
Since this recipe requires precise techniques, we recommend that either a commercially available puff pastry crust is substituted for the top crust or that the raspberries are baked as a traditional pie with the cream and egg white mixture served as an accompanying sauce after the pie is baked and cooled.

Grape Pie

INGREDIENTS

4 cups Concord grapes
1 cup granulated sugar
2 1/2 teaspoons quick-cooking tapioca
1/2 teaspoon salt
2 teaspoons grated orange rind
1/2 teaspoon grated lemon rind
1 tablespoon butter
Pie Crust (p. 160)

Method
Slip skins from grapes; reserve skins. Bring pulp to a boil and cook until seeds loosen from pulp; remove from heat; cool slightly. Press through a colander or sieve to remove seeds. Combine grape pulp, reserved skins, sugar, tapioca, salt, and orange and lemon rinds. Let stand 20 minutes to thicken. Spoon into prepared pie crust; dot with butter. Top with lattice crust or prepared pie crust. Bake at 450 degrees for 10 minutes. Reduce temperature to 350 degrees; continue baking for 20 to 25 minutes or until crust is golden brown.

Yield
Makes 1 9-inch pie.

Prune Pie

1 pound pitted prunes
1 lemon, quartered
6 large shredded wheat biscuits, lightly toasted
Milk or half and half
Heavy cream, whipped

Method
In a medium saucepan, combine prunes and lemon; add enough water to cover fruit; sweeten to taste. Simmer 20 minutes or until prunes are tender. Drain, reserving about 1/4 cup liquid; discard lemon. Quarter prunes. Dip shredded wheat in milk or half and half; arrange on serving dish and drizzle with reserved prune liquid. Top with cut-up prunes. Serve topped with whipped cream.

Yield
Makes 6 servings.

Note
Can arrange the biscuits in a 1 1/2-quart shallow dish or into 6 individual bowls.

Banana Cream

INGREDIENTS
Ripe bananas
Pinch of salt
Heavy cream, whipped
Powdered sugar
Blanched almonds
Candied cherries

Method
Peel bananas and mash or press through a sieve; add salt. For each cup of mashed fruit, stir in 1 cup whipped cream. For each cup of whipped cream and banana mixture, fold in 2 tablespoons powdered sugar. Spoon into serving dishes; top with almonds and cherries. Serve immediately.

Steamed Banana Pudding

INGREDIENTS

3 eggs
1 cup granulated sugar
1 tablespoon water
2 teaspoons baking powder
1 cup flour
2 bananas sliced

Method
Beat together eggs and sugar until well blended; stir in water. Combine baking powder and flour; beat into egg mixture until smooth. Stir in sliced bananas. Fill 8 6-ounce custard cups or individual oven-proof dessert dishes half full. Set dishes in water bath. Bake at 325 degrees for 40 to 45 minutes or until wooden pick inserted in center comes out clean. Serve warm or chilled.

Yield
Makes 8 servings.

Banana Blanc Mange

INGREDIENTS

3 tablespoons cornstarch
3 tablespoons granulated sugar
2 tablespoons cold milk
1 quart milk
3 bananas, sliced

Method
Combine cornstarch and sugar; stir in 2 tablespoons cold milk, mixing until smooth. In a 4-quart saucepan, heat quart of milk just to boiling; slowly add cornstarch mixture, stirring constantly. Continue simmering, stirring constantly, until thickened. Remove from heat; stir to cool. Stir in sliced bananas. Pour into serving bowl. Chill.

Yield
Makes 8 to 10 servings.

Baked Bananas

INGREDIENTS

Bananas
Granulated sugar
Lemon juice
Water

Method
Peel bananas and split in half lengthwise. Scoop out center seeds. Arrange bananas in baking dish; sprinkle with sugar and drizzle with lemon juice. Add a small amount of water to dish, about 1/4 cup. Bake at 375 degrees for 20 to 30 minutes or until bananas are tender.

Cream Puffs

INGREDIENTS
1/2 cup butter
1 cup water
1 cup flour
3 eggs

Filling
1 cup granulated sugar
4 tablespoons cornstarch
2 cups milk
2 eggs
1/2 teaspoon vanilla (optional)

Method
In medium saucepan, melt butter in boiling water. While water is still boiling, add flour all at once and stir vigorously until mixture forms a ball. Remove from heat and cool slightly. Add eggs one at a time, beating well after each. For each large cream puff, drop about 1/4 cup batter onto greased baking sheet. (For petite cream puffs, use about 1 tablespoon batter). Bake at 450 degrees for 15 minutes; reduce heat to 325 degrees and continue baking for 20 to 25 minutes or until golden brown. Remove from oven and split immediately to vent steam.

Filling: In medium saucepan, combine sugar and cornstarch; stir in milk. Cook over medium heat, stirring constantly, until thickened. Lightly beat eggs in a small bowl, then stir in a small amount of the hot mixture. Return egg mixture to saucepan and continue cooking, stirring constantly, for an additional 2 minutes. Cool completely; stir in vanilla, if desired. Fill Cream Puffs.

Yield
Makes 10 large or 20 to 24 petite cream puffs.

Cream Cakes (Popovers)

INGREDIENTS

2 eggs
1 cup milk
1 cup flour
1/2 teaspoon salt

Filling
2 tablespoons granulated sugar
2 tablespoons cornstarch
1 1/2 cups milk
1/4 teaspoon salt
1 egg
1/2 teaspoon vanilla

Method
Beat together eggs and milk with a wire whisk or rotary beater. Beat in flour and salt until blended to a smooth batter. If lumps remain, pour through a sieve or strainer. Fill 8 to 10 well-greased popover pans or custard cups half full with batter. Bake at 475 degrees for 15 minutes; reduce heat to 350 degrees and continue baking for 25 minutes or until golden brown. A few minutes before removing from oven, prick to vent steam.

Filling: In medium saucepan, combine sugar, cornstarch, and salt; stir in milk. Cook over medium heat, stirring constantly, until thickened. Lightly beat egg in a small bowl, then stir in a small amount of the hot mixture. Return egg mixture to saucepan and continue cooking, stirring constantly, for an additional 2 minutes. Stir in vanilla. Cool completely. Fill Cream Cakes.

Yield
Makes 8 large or 10 medium cream cakes.

Button Cookies

1 pound butter (4 sticks), softened
2 cups granulated sugar
3 eggs
2 tablespoons bourbon whiskey
1 tablespoon lemon juice
6 to 8 cups flour
2 teaspoons baking powder
Additional granulated sugar
Cinnamon
Whole blanched almonds

Method
Cream butter and sugar until light and fluffy. Beat in eggs, whiskey, and lemon juice. Combine flour and baking powder. Add flour mixture to butter and egg mixture, mixing to form a stiff dough. Shape into 1-inch balls; roll in sugar mixed with small amount of cinnamon. Press almond into center of each cookie. Place on greased baking sheet. Bake at 375 degrees for 12 to 15 minutes or until lightly browned.

Yield
Makes about 12 dozen cookies.

Anise Cookies

4 cups powdered sugar
6 eggs, beaten
2 tablespoons crushed anise seeds
3 1/2 to 4 cups flour
Additional powdered sugar for dusting

Method
Beat powdered sugar into eggs until foamy. Add anise seeds and flour, mixing to form a stiff dough. Dough will be somewhat sticky. Refrigerate several hours for better handling, if desired. Shape into 1-inch balls. Place on greased baking sheet. Bake at 325 degrees for 12 minutes or until lightly browned around edges. Dust with powdered sugar. Store in air-tight container.

Yield
Makes about 6 dozen cookies.

Note
This is a crisp, somewhat dry cookie.

Brown Cookies

2 cups packed brown sugar
5 eggs
2 ounces unsweetened chocolate, melted
2 cups flour
1 teaspoon cinnamon
2 1/2 teaspoons baking powder
1 cup chopped dates or candied citron
1/2 cup slivered almonds

Method
Beat sugar into eggs. Stir in melted chocolate. Combine flour, cinnamon, baking powder, and dates or citron; add to sugar and egg mixture, mixing until blended. Stir in almonds. Spread into a greased and floured 10 1/2- x 15 1/2- x 1-inch jelly roll pan. Bake at 375 degrees for 20 minutes. Cool. Cut into 1 1/2-inch squares.

Yield
Makes about 6 dozen squares.

Note
These are traditional German bar cookies, much like gingerbread cake.

Broiled Chicken

1 2 1/2- to 3-pound broiler-fryer chicken, cut-up
Melted butter
Salt
Black pepper

Method
Brush chicken pieces with melted butter; sprinkle with salt and
pepper. Arrange chicken, skin-side down, on broiler pan. Broil,
4 to 6 inches from heat source, for 15 to 20 minutes on each
side, turning at least once and basting with additional butter as
needed, until chicken is cooked and juices run clear.

Yield
Makes 4 to 6 servings.

Hamburg Steak

1 pound lean ground beef
2 teaspoons onion juice
1/2 teaspoon salt
1/4 teaspoon black pepper
1 tablespoon flour
1 cup beef broth
1 tablespoon catsup
1 teaspoon Worcestershire sauce
1 tablespoon chopped parsley

Method
Combine beef, onion juice, salt, and pepper; mix lightly. Shape into 4 round patties. Fry patties in hot skillet over medium-high heat until browned on both sides and thoroughly cooked. Place patties on heated serving platter. Stir flour into 1 tablespoon reserved pan drippings. Add broth, stirring to deglaze pan. Bring to boil; cook, stirring constantly until thickened. Stir in catsup, Worcestershire sauce, and parsley. Pour over meat patties.

Yield
Makes 4 servings.

Tomato Soup

INGREDIENTS
1 tablespoon butter
1 tablespoon flour
2 cups milk
1 cup tomato juice
1/2 teaspoon baking soda
Salt

Method
In medium saucepan, melt butter and add flour; stir in milk. Cook over medium heat, stirring constantly, until thickened. Stir in tomato juice and baking soda. Season to taste. Heat thoroughly.

Yield
Makes 4 servings.

Spanish Cream

2 cups plus 2 tablespoons milk, divided
2 egg yolks
2 tablespoons granulated sugar
2 teaspoons unflavored gelatin (1 envelope)
2 egg whites, beaten to stiff peaks
1/2 teaspoon vanilla (optional)

Method

In a saucepan over medium heat, heat milk just to steaming. Mix together egg yolks and sugar. Stir a small amount of hot milk into the egg mixture. Return to pan; continue cooking for 2 minutes. In a medium bowl, soften gelatin in 2 tablespoons milk. Add heated milk mixture to gelatin, stirring until gelatin dissolves. Stir in vanilla, if desired. Stir to cool to room temperature. Fold in beaten egg whites. Pour into serving bowl. Chill until set.

Yield
Makes 6 to 8 servings.

Chocolate Blanc Mange

2 teaspoons unflavored gelatin (1 envelope)
2 1/4 cups milk, divided
1/4 cup granulated sugar
2 tablespoons cocoa

Method
In medium mixing bowl, soften gelatin in 1/4 cup milk. Combine sugar and cocoa in a saucepan. Add remaining 2 cups milk, and heat, stirring just until sugar dissolves and milk is steaming. Pour heated milk over softened gelatin, stirring until gelatin is dissolved. Stir to cool. Pour into 6 4-ounce serving dishes. Chill until set.

Yield
Makes 6 servings.

Asparagus Soup

1 pound fresh asparagus, cut into 2-inch pieces
4 cups water
1 cup half and half
1 teaspoon salt
1/4 cup butter
2 teaspoons cornstarch

Method
Cook asparagus in boiling water until very tender. Drain, reserving liquid. In saucepan, combine reserved liquid, half and half, salt, and butter. Bring to a boil; add cornstarch combined with 1 tablespoon cold water. Cook, stirring constantly, until thickened. Puree asparagus in blender or food mill; stir into mixture in pan. Heat thoroughly. May be served hot or cold.

Yield
Makes 6 to 8 servings.

Eggnog

INGREDIENTS

1 egg yolk, chilled
1 tablespoon granulated sugar
1 tablespoon whiskey or brandy
1 scant cup (8 ounces) whole milk

Method
Beat the egg yolk until foamy. Continue to beat, while gradually adding sugar. Slowly stir in liquor, then milk. Chill again before serving.

Yield
Makes 1 serving.

NOTES

Texts citing *Manufacturer and Builder, Century, North American Review, Atlantic Monthly, Scientific American, New Series, New Englander and Yale Review,* and *Scribner's Monthly* are available from the Cornell University Making of America Digital Collection online. Texts citing the *Chicago Daily Tribune* are available through ProQuest Historical Newspapers.

Preface

1. Mitchell, "Cookbooks."
2. Joselit, "A Set Table," 21.
3. Zeitlin, *Germans in Wisconsin,* 37, 43.
4. By the 1880s approximately 90 percent of the Jews in America were Reform. Heller, *Isaac M. Wise,* contains the text of the Pittsburgh Platform of 1885 (464–65). Irma too joined a Reform congregation in Chicago upon her marriage. Her involvement in Jewish life and the Jewish community is demonstrated in a number of other ways: her volunteer work for the Jewish Kopperl Relief Agency during 1892–93, her teaching of the Sabbath school at Rabbi Bernard Felsenthal's Zion Congregation, along with her participation in the Isaiah Temple sisterhood, where she rose to its presidency, and her work for the philanthropic Chicago Jewish Woman's Aid Society. See also Berrol, "Class or Ethnicity."
5. Frankenstein, *Irma,* 201n5. David Einhorn (1809–79) was born in Bavaria. He was one of the early and most radical rabbinical proponents of Reform Judaism. He pushed to have Jewish services in the vernacular. After he came to the United States,

he influenced the 1869 Philadelphia Rabbinical Conference to adopt a radical Reform platform. See Kaufman Kohler, *Gates of Jewish Heritage.*

6. Frankenstein, *Irma,* 201–2n8.

7. Irma chose not to keep kosher in her own home. She never specified any recipe as a holiday-specific food; none of the recipes she included in her cookbook required kosher preparation, products, fish, poultry, or meats.

8. FitzSimmons, *Teach Me,* 7–8.

Introduction

1. Irma Rosenthal Frankenstein, undated papers, ca. 1953, Irma Rosenthal Frankenstein Papers, Chicago Jewish Archives, Spertus Institute of Jewish Studies (hereafter cited as IRF); Frankenstein, *Irma,* 66 (ca. 1953).

2. IRF, loose paper associated with notebook, undated entry, ca. 1953.

3. The full quote reads, "I say again, man cannot choose his duties. You may choose to forsake your duties, and choose not to have the sorrow they bring. But you will go forth; and what will you find, my daughter? Sorrow without duty—bitter herbs, and no bread with them." Eliot, *Romola,* 2:432; Frankenstein, *Irma,* 69 (ca. 1953).

4. IRF, undated entry, 1953. The quote Irma paraphrased comes from Henry David Thoreau's chapter "Where I Lived, and What I Lived For," in *Walden.* The actual quote reads, "To affect the quality of the day, that is the highest of arts" (90).

Chapter 1

1. Bancroft, *Book of the Fair,* 885.

2. Rippley, *Immigrant Experience,* 174.

3. Faust, *German Element,* 1:587, 589.

4. Ade, *Stories of Chicago,* 75.

5. Adams, *Deutsche im Schmeltztiegel,* 38; translation by E. Reichman and L. J. Rippley, for the IUPUI Max Kade German-American Institute, Indiana University-Purdue University at Indianapolis (1993): www.ulib.iupui.edu/kade/adams/cover. html. See also Quentin, *Reisebilder und Studien,* part 2, for the

author's impressions gathered during a six-month stay in the United States in 1850, covering the cities of Chicago, Milwaukee, St. Louis, and Cincinnati.

6. IRF, Saturday, August 29, 1953.

7. Cutler, *Jews of Chicago,* 19–20. See also Brinkmann, *Von der Gemeinde zur "Community",* for an excellent discussion of the various German Jewish groups who made their home in Chicago and their efforts to maintain their Jewish identity and to establish community.

8. The Pittsburgh Platform of 1885 made eight declarations of principles—guidelines defining modern Judaism. Item 4 stated: "We hold that all such Mosaic and rabbinical laws as regulate diet, priestly purity, and dress originated in ages and under the influence of ideas entirely foreign to our present mental and spiritual state. They fail to impress the modern Jew with a spirit of priestly holiness; their observance in our days is apt rather to obstruct than to further modern spiritual elevation." Irma's parents were among the early adherents of the Jewish reform movement. Rabbi Bernard Felsenthal, a family friend of the Rosenthal's, had been one of the leaders of the Reform conference in Philadelphia in 1869, which set the stage for the later Pittsburgh Platform.

9. McWilliams, *Mask for Privilege,* 19–20.

10. IRF, undated entry, ca. 1953; IRF, Tuesday, August 25, 1953.

11. The term *Kleindeutschland* is from Hense-Jensen and Bruncken, *Wisconsins Deutsch-Amerikaner,* 1:140.

12. IRF, Monday, August 24, 1953.

13. Zeitlin, *Germans in Wisconsin,* 21.

14. Hoobler and Hoobler, *German American Family Album,* 77.

15. IRF, Friday, September 4, 1953; Frankenstein, *Irma,* 198 (ca. 1944). Irma's reference to John Ruskin is from his 1875 work *The Ethics of the Dust: Ten Lectures to Little Housewives on the Elements of Crystallization,* lecture 7, "Home Virtues."

16. Frankenstein, *Irma,* 11 (Friday, March 28, 1958); IRF, Saturday, August 29, 1953; IRF, undated entry, 1953.

17. Levenstein, *Revolution at the Table,* 163. See also Crumpacker, *Old-Time Brand-Name Cookbook.*

18. Faust, *German Element,* 2:463.

19. Young, "Hampton Reminiscences."

20. Rundell, *Experienced American Housekeeper.*

21. Review of *American Woman's Home; or, Principles of Domestic Science,* by Catharine Beecher and Harriet Beecher Stowe, *Manufacturer and Builder* 1, no. 7 (1869): 214.

22. Notices of New Books, *Principles of Domestic Science,* by Catharine Beecher and Harriet Beecher Stowe, *New Englander and Yale Review* 29, no. 111 (1870): 366.

23. Davidis's cookbook has recently been republished as *Pickled Herring and Pumpkin Pie.*

24. Max Kade Institute, "Story of Immigration."

25. Theophano, "Recipes for Reverie."

26. "The Art of Cooking," *Manufacturer and Builder* 10, no. 9 (1878): 211.

27. IRF, undated entry, 1953.

28. Shapiro, *Perfection Salad,* 38.

29. Ibid., 35.

30. Rury, "Vocationalism for Home and Work," 24–25, 27.

31. Shapiro, *Perfection Salad,* 65.

32. Ibid., 39.

33. Moritz and Kahn, *Twentieth Century Cook Book,* 1.

34. Frankenstein, *Irma,* 158 (Friday, September 28, 1951).

35. IRF, Saturday, May 31, 1958.

Chapter 2

1. IRF, undated entry, 1953; IRF, Saturday, August 29, 1953.

2. IRF, Tuesday, August 25, 1953.

3. Max Kade Institute, "Kaffee- und Teegesellschaften."

4. Levy, *Jewish Cookery Book,* 3.

5. Frankenstein, *Irma,* 68 (undated entry, ca. 1953).

6. Zobrowski and Herzog, *Life Is with People,* 372–73.

7. Holly, "Ensuring Freshness."

8. Wright, *Annual Report, 1903,* 719.

9. See Moritz and Kahn, *Twentieth Century Cook Book,* 279–80, for other traditional German tortes.

10. I. D. Bullard, "Domestic Science, Lesson No. 154—Yeast," *Chicago Daily Tribune,* January 31, 1904.

11. Croly, *Jennie June's American Cookery Book,* 353.

12. Atwater, "The Digestibility of Food," 739. See also Pereira, "Treatise on Food and Diet," 26.

13. Bancroft, *Book of the Fair,* 286.

14. "Will Show How to Make Bread," *Chicago Daily Tribune*, June 4, 1893.
15. Front dustjacket flyleaf of the reprint edition of Levy, *Jewish Cookery Book*.
16. *Chicago Record*, June 10, 1899.
17. The *Chicago Daily Tribune* also cost two cents and published recipes as well.
18. "Banana Flour Is New," *Chicago Daily Tribune*, August 12, 1898. See Lincoln, *Mrs. Lincoln's Boston Cook Book*, 42, for a discussion about how "health-food flour," or whole-wheat flour, is made and its nutritional value. See Farmer, *Boston Cooking-School Cook Book*, 49–52, for a discussion about various kinds of flour and their production.
19. In the abstract of a paper, "Adulterations of Food," presented before the meeting of the American Social Science Association, at Saratoga, New York, Professor S. W. Johnson listed these common adulterants found in bread flour.
20. See "Educational Chicago," *Chicago Daily Tribune*, September 7, 1890, for cadet teachers' salary rates that apparently remained unchanged until 1899.
21. Wright, *Annual Report, 1903*, 693, 749.

Chapter 3

1. Wright, *Annual Report, 1903*, 262–97, 679.
2. Irma often spelled German words phonetically. The correct spelling is *soße*.
3. Wright, *Annual Report, 1903*, 807.
4. Atkinson, "Art of Cooking."
5. Farmer, *Boston Cooking-School Cook Book*, 206.
6. Shapiro, *Perfection Salad*, 86–87.
7. *Chicago Daily Tribune*, May 1, 1898:34.
8. "Martha's Management," *Chicago Record*, April 3, 1899.
9. IRF, Thursday, June 17, 1937.
10. Leviticus 2:14, 23:14; Joshua 5:11; Ruth 2:14; 1 Samuel 17:17, 25:18; 2 Samuel 17:28. In Ruth 2:14, roasted wheat is mentioned as being eaten at the time of the barley harvest.
11. Bogue, *Fishing the Great Lakes*, 162, 164–66, 255, 256.
12. Carp were not native to the United States. See Wisconsin Sea Grant, "Fish of the Great Lakes: Carp."

13. Krasner-Khait, "The Impact of Refrigeration."
14. Fresh whitefish cost approximately twelve cents per pound in 1898. Wright, *Annual Report, 1903*, 741.
15. Joselit, "A Set Table," 22.
16. Kirshenblatt-Gimblett, "Kitchen Judaism," 78–80.
17. Atwater, "Pecuniary Economy of Food," 440.
18. See "Diet Kitchen" (1892 circular), Jane Addams Memorial Collection, reel 50:1724–25, Special Collections, University Library, University of Illinois at Chicago. The cost of oyster soup was fifteen cents per quart or ten cents per pint. "Golden Gate Oysters Brought from the Atlantic," *Chicago Record*, July 16, 1893:12. The article also states that live Atlantic oysters were first brought across the United States in 1870, when the transcontinental railway was completed.
19. Parker, *Handbook for Mothers*, 107.
20. *Chicago Record Cook Book*, iv.
21. Dyspepsia, or indigestion, was a common complaint during Victorian times and later.

Chapter 4

1. The Boston Store advertisement, *Chicago Daily Tribune*, January 16, 1898: 43. See also Wright, *Annual Report, 1903*, 733.
2. Rorer, *Made-Over Dishes*, preface.
3. "King Steer Still Rules," *Chicago Daily Tribune*, March, 26, 1899: C2.
4. Farmer, *Boston Cooking-School Cook Book*, 92.
5. Atwater, "How Food Nourishes," 240.
6. Atwater, "Digestibility of Food," 735.
7. Rorer, *Made-Over Dishes*, under "Eggs."
8. "Summer Dishes and Drinks," *Chicago Daily Tribune*, July 7, 1895:33.
9. "How to Make Salads," *Chicago Daily Tribune*, June 2, 1895:46.
10. Shapiro, *Perfection Salad*, 92, 94.
11. "Art in Decorating Dishes," *Chicago Daily Tribune*, January 1, 1898:24.
12. "Dainty Summer Salads," *Chicago Daily Tribune*, August 22, 1898:16; advertisement for Paine's Celery Compound, *Chicago Daily Tribune*, April 25, 1897:6.
13. *Chicago Record Cook Book*, 335. The "Martha's Management"

column in the *Chicago Record* hailed celery as "one of the most valuable vegetables containing an essential oil" (April 3, 1899).

14. "Chestnuts Very Quiet," *Chicago Record,* January 19, 1899:8.

15. Krasner-Khait, "Impact of Refrigeration." See also "Outlook for Michigan Berries," *Chicago Daily Tribune,* May 15, 1898:34.

16. James, *Portrait of a Lady,* 585.

17. The *Chicago Daily Tribune* frequently reported fashionable events, including afternoon teas, given and attended by Chicago's upper classes. See, e.g., "Other Notable Social Events," *Chicago Daily Tribune,* January 1, 1897:7. Regarding appropriate attire, behavior, and manners at tea parties, see "Concerning Tea Gowns and Jackets," *Chicago Daily Tribune,* January 3, 1897:32; "A Velvet Tea Gown" (drawing), *Chicago Daily Tribune,* January 13, 1898:8; Beezley, *Our Manners;* and Cooke, *Social Etiquette.*

18. IRF, Monday, May 12, 1958.

19. E. Kellogg, *Science in the Kitchen,* 468.

20. "For the Home Woman," *Chicago Record,* May 5, 1889:8.

21. "A Bunch of Receipts," *New York Times,* December 30, 1894:18.

22. Vaughan's Seeds display advertisement, *Chicago Daily Tribune,* May 9, 1899:5. For the price of raisins, see retail grocer display ad, *Chicago Daily Tribune,* January 15, 1899:10. For the price of peanuts, recipes containing peanuts, and their benefits for anemics, see "Nut Grows in Favor," *Chicago Daily Tribune,* July 30, 1899:39.

23. "Making Salads of Nasturtiums," *New York Times,* January 19, 1896:15.

24. Shapiro, *Perfection Salad,* 129. A Siegel-Cooper and Company ad in the *Chicago Daily Tribune,* March 5, 1899, offered one dozen naval oranges from California for twenty-four cents.

25. "Culture and Progress," *Scribner's Monthly* 10, no. 4 (1875): 515–24, quote from 517–18.

26. "Fruits as Food," *Manufacturer and Builder* 22, no. 4 (1890): 91–92, qtd. from *Good Housekeeping,* n.d.

27. Latcha, "Railroads versus Canals," 220.

28. See, e.g., the daily produce reports in *Chicago Record,* page 8; the same California prunes were a little less than eight cents per pound in 1898 according to Wright, *Annual Report,* 1903, 813.

29. See H. R. Eagle display advertisement for tinned blackberries, *Chicago Daily Tribune,* February 20, 1898:28. See also report on wholesale prices, *Chicago Daily Tribune,* July 17, 1898:30.

30. See display advertisement for Charles H. Slack, Grocer, *Chicago Daily Tribune*, August 11, 1898:11.

31. See Frank Brothers display advertisement, *Chicago Daily Tribune*, January 1, 1898:29.

32. Soluri, "Accounting for Taste," 386.

33. "Fruit Farms in Cellars," *Chicago Daily Tribune*, February 7, 1897:38.

34. *The New England Farmer: A Monthly Journal Devoted to Agriculture, Horticulture, and Their Kindred Arts and Sciences* (Market Street, Boston) contained agricultural and horticultural information, as well as recipes.

35. Frankenstein, *Irma*, 181 (Thursday, December 18, 1931).

36. IRF, Friday, May 23, 1958; IRF, Wednesday, August 19, 1953.

37. IRF, Wednesday, November 17, 1937; IRF, Tuesday, March 11, 1941.

38. During the years she wrote about specific dishes that she prepared (primarily between 1930–40), Irma mentioned making creamed foods (mushrooms, chicken patties, Chicken à la King, salmon, potatoes, and celery) a mere six times.

Chapter 5

1. IRF, undated entry, ca. 1953. The connection between malnutrition and tuberculosis (consumption) was mentioned in an advertisement for *Dr. Pierce's Common Sense Medical Advisor, Chicago Daily Tribune* (March 27, 1899:51). The book touted the benefits of Pierce's patent medicines: Golden Medical Discovery and Pleasant Pellets for consumption, pneumonia, and diarrheal diseases.

2. Centers for Disease Control and Prevention, "Achievements in Public Health," 621.

3. Ibid., 622.

4. "The Price of Life and Health," *Manufacturer and Builder* 22, no. 1 (1890):19.

5. Diner, *Hungering for America*, 35.

6. Chicken (dressed hens) was around ten cents per pound in 1898, according to Wright, *Annual Report, 1903,* 713. See "Salisbury Steak," *Chicago Daily Tribune*, January 24, 1885:6; Salisbury, *Relation*, 97–98.

7. Davidis, *Pickled Herring,* 104. See "Cooking in Germany," *New*

York Times, November 7, 1880:4.

8. Reynolds, "Dr. Neeley's Report," 21–23.

9. "Yelk" was an alternate spelling of "yolk." The spellings were used interchangeably; both were considered correct. The culinary columnist for the *Chicago Record* between 1892 and 1899 consistently used "yolk," but during that same time frame, the *Chicago Daily Tribune* culinary editor preferred "yelk."

10. Bunny Crumpacker places the beginning of the Knox Gelatin Company in 1890. *Old-Time Brand-Name Cookbook,* xvii. In 1894 Knox introduced Sparkling Granulated Calves Foot Gelatine.

11. Typhoid and malarial fevers had a hugely negative impact on the liver, and so, given that asparagus was thought to be a "Liver-Regulating 'Grass,'" it made sense to prescribe asparagus soup for the fever victims. "Asparagus in Abundance," *Chicago Record,* May 20, 1899:8. See also advertisement for "Dr. Hobbs Sparagus Kidney Pills," purported to make the kidneys strong and healthful, especially benefiting malaria sufferers, *Chicago Daily Tribune,* March 8, 1896:13.

12. A free cookbook was offered for the price of a stamped envelope on the back pages of the *Atlantic Monthly,* December 1896. It promised "specially contributed receipts by Marion Harland, Miss Maria Parloa, Mrs. S. T. Rorer, Mrs. D. A. Lincoln, Mrs. Eliza R. Parker, and nearly fifty other leading teachers of cookery and writers on Domestic Science" among its seventy-eight pages. Also an advertisement for Durkee's salad dressing in the back pages of the *Century,* April 1899, offered a free booklet: "'Salads: How to Make and Dress These,' giving many valuable and novel recipes for Salads, Sandwiches, Sauces, Luncheon Dishes, etc."

13. Theophano, *Eat My Words,* 267.

14. Parloa, "The New England Kitchen." In 1898 Maria Parloa authored a cookbook called *Home Economics: A Guide to Household Management* (New York: Century), and she also wrote food and nutrition columns for the *Ladies Home Journal.*

15. Richards, "Rumford Kitchen Exhibit." In Edward Atkinson's 1896 book, *The Science of Nutrition,* Richards explains the rationale for naming the kitchen after Count Rumford: it was to celebrate "the 100th anniversary of Count Rumford's work in Bavaria and Italy, which was the birth of the Science of Nutri-

tion, as he himself called it" (198). In 1899 Richards gave a more extensive account of Count Rumford and his experiments in "Count Rumford and His Work for Humanity."

16. E. Kellogg, *Science in the Kitchen*, 3.

17. See "Distress Relieved at Kopperl's," *Chicago Daily Tribune*, September 7, 1893:1.

18. "Hull-House Kitchen," undated circular, ca. 1891, Jane Addams Memorial Collection, reel 50:1696. James F. Case's recipe for Case's Health Bread is given in Atkinson, *The Science of Nutrition*, 64–65. Case's Health Bread is also mentioned as being made in the New England Kitchen; see Abel, "Study in Social Economics," 138.

19. "Diet Kitchen," 1892 circular, Jane Addams Memorial Collection, reel 50:1724–25.

20. Addams, *Twenty Years at Hull-House*, 130–31. Harvey Levenstein writes that "the possibility of expansion to Chicago opened when Julia Lathrop, another student of Ellen Richards at MIT, accepted a post at Hull House. Before Lathrop left for Chicago, Mary Abel trained her in the ways of the NEK [New England Kitchen]. At Hull House she opened a 'people's kitchen' patterned on the New York and Boston ones." "New England Kitchen," 378. However, Diane Dillon states, "Hull-House resident Annie Lathrop [Hull-House resident Julia Lathrop's sister] went to Boston to study scientific food preparation with Richards and Abel." "Hull-House Experiments."

21. Addams, "Objective Value."

22. "Pure Food for Pupils: Hygienic Luncheons Planned," *Chicago Daily Tribune*, May 26, 1899:8.

23. See display ad for the Battle Creek Sanitarium Health Food Company, *Chicago Record*, May 7, 1899:31.

24. A search in the archives of the *Chicago Daily Tribune* between January 1, 1898, and December 31, 1899 produced no fewer than eighty articles dealing with vegetarians and vegetarianism. These items ranged from the May 25, 1899, mention of a new vegetarian café, possibly run by the Battle Creek Health Food Company, in the downtown Chicago area ("The Progress of Vegetarianism") to the proselytizing "Man Naturally a Vegetarian" (February 5, 1899) to the sarcastic "Fighting Vegetarians" (April 23, 1898). Kellogg purportedly did not become aware of soybeans until much later than 1899, with his first mention

of the bean appearing in *The New Method in Diabetes* (1917). However, if the interview did concern the Battle Creek Sanitarium Health Food Company store in Chicago, which sold foods produced under Kellogg's auspices and approved by him, he may have been aware of the soybean earlier than is commonly supposed. See J. Kellogg, *New Method in Diabetes*. See also W. Shurtleff and A. Aoyagi, "Dr. John Harvey Kellogg and Battle Creek Foods: Work with Soy," *The Soy Daily*, www.thesoydaily.com/MOS/adventist02.csf.

25. Dowling, "Old School Medicine," 592.

26. "A Chicago Invalid" to the city editor, *Chicago Daily Tribune*, March 24, 1898:8.

27. "Baking-Powders," *Manufacturer and Builder* 2, no. 3 (1870):88.

28. Ted Hymowitz, professor of plant genetics at the University of Illinois at Urbana–Champaign, personal communication, September 20, 2004; William Shurtleff, director of the Soyfoods Center, personal communication, September, 21, 2004. See also Jane Eddington's column "Tribune Cook Book," *Chicago Daily Tribune*, March 21, 1917, which states, "Soy, or soja bean, as they are labeled in some shops, are made into a flour for diabetics by one medical manufactory in the country."

29. Haberlandt, *Die Sojabohne*, part 4, 106; translation courtesy of William Shurtleff.

30. Thompson, "Soja Beans," 141.

31. F. Matthews, "Great Is Kaffir Corn," *Harper's Weekly*, March 19, 1898, reprinted in *Chicago Daily Tribune*, May 21, 1898, 4.

32. "Aerated Bread," *Manufacturer and Builder*, 26, no. 11 (1894): 258. The process had been invented by Dr. Dauglish, an Edinburgh physician, in 1859. An aerated bread factory was also established in Boston in 1860. The bakery in San Francisco opened in 1862 according to a notice titled "Aerated Bread in California," in the *Scientific American,* September 20, 1862:186. Kendal's Aerated Bread Bakery was located at the southwest corner of Dearborn and Washington streets in Chicago around 1865, according to W. E. Hagans, "In the Wake of the News," *Chicago Daily Tribune*, May 8, 1934:25. See also, Farmer, *Boston Cooking-School Cook Book,* 57.

33. E. Kellogg, *Science in the Kitchen,* 164–216, esp. 212.

34. The discovery of saccharin was jointly published by Ira Remsen and Constantine Fahlberg in 1880, according to James Stimpert

in "Ira Remsen: The Chemistry was Right," *Gazette Online*, September 11, 2000, www.jhu.edu/~gazette/2000/sep1100/.

35. "A New Sugar Substitute," *Manufacturer and Builder*, 20, no. 7 (1888):147.

36. "Talks of Cinnamic Cure," *Chicago Daily Tribune*, December 17, 1898:6. For data about cinnamon's use in ivory jelly, see the Natural Care website: www.naturalcareonline.com/p6.php?herbdataPage=9.

37. E. Kellogg, *Science in the Kitchen*, 31.

38. Lincoln, "Extracts from Cookery," 141, 142.

39. E. Kellogg, *Science in the Kitchen*, 22.

40. To trace the efforts of the Chicago Kitchen Garden Association, a private charitable organization founded in 1883, to train young girls in the arts of cooking and homemaking and to have this curriculum adopted in Chicago public schools, see *Chicago Daily Tribune*, February 1, 1891:4; May 24, 1891:6; December 11, 1897:10; January 15, 1898:4; March 19, 1898:10. When the University of Chicago opened in 1892, the curriculum included courses in the section of sanitary science under the Department of Social Science and Anthropology, according to Dye, *Home Economics*, 11. Many graduates of this program worked as nutritionists and home economics teachers in the Chicago public school system and other Cook County institutions.

41. Frankenstein, *Irma*, 69 (Sunday, May 9, 1948).

42. IRF, Wednesday, April 23, 1958; IRF, Thursday, May 22, 1958.

Bibliography

Manuscript Collections

Addams, Jane. Memorial Collection. Special Collections, University Library, University of Illinois at Chicago.

Frankenstein, Irma Rosenthal. Papers. Chicago Jewish Archives, Spertus Institute of Jewish Studies. Collection No. 262, Accession No. 2004–5.

Published Sources

Abel, M. H. "A Study in Social Economics: The Story of the New England Kitchen." In *Plain Words about Food: The Rumford Kitchen Leaflets,* ed. E. H. Richards, 135–54. Boston: Rockwell and Church Press, 1899.

Adams, W. P. *Deutsche im Schmeltztiegel der USA: Erfahrungen im größten Einwanderungsland der Europäer.* Berlin: Die Ausländerbeauftragte des Senats, 1990.

Addams, J. "The Objective Value of a Social Settlement." In *Philanthropy and Social Progress: Seven Essays,* 27–56. New York: T. Y. Crowell, 1893.

———. *Twenty Years at Hull-House with Autobiographical Notes.* New York: MacMillan, 1912.

Ade, G. *Stories of Chicago,* ed. F. J. Meine. Urbana: University of Illinois Press, 2003.

American Type Founders Company. *Specimens of Type: Brass Rules and Dashes, Ornaments and Borders, Society Emblems, Check Lines, Cuts, Initials and Other Productions of the American Type Founders Company.* 1896. Reprint, New York: Garland, 1981.

Atkinson, E. "The Art of Cooking." *Manufacturer and Builder* 22 (January 1890): 18–19.

——. "The Art of Cooking." In *Manufacturer and Builder* 22 (February 1890): 40–41.

——. *The Science of Nutrition: Treatise upon the Science of Nutrition, the Aladdin Oven.* Boston: Damrell and Upham, 1896.

Atwater, W. O. "The Digestibility of Food." *The Century* 34, no. 5 (1887): 733–40.

——. "How Food Nourishes the Body: The Chemistry of Food, II." *The Century* 34, no. 2 (1887): 237–52.

——. "Pecuniary Economy of Food." *The Century* 35, no. 3 (1888): 437–46.

Bancroft, H. H. *The Book of the Fair: An Historical and Descriptive Presentation of the World's Science, Art, and Industry, as Viewed through the Columbian Exposition at Chicago in 1893.* Edition Cygne Noir. Chicago: Bancroft, 1893.

Beecher, C. E., and H. B. Stowe. *The American Woman's Home; or, Principles of Domestic Science: Being a Guide to the Formation and Maintenance of Economical, Healthful, Beautiful, and Christian Homes.* New York: J. D. Ford, 1869.

Beezley, C. F. *Our Manners and Social Customs: A Practical Guide to Deportment, Easy Manners, and Social Etiquette.* Philadelphia: Elliott and Beezley, 1891.

Berrol, S. "Class or Ethnicity: The Americanized German Jewish Woman and Her Middle Class Sisters in 1895." *Jewish Social Studies* 47, no. 1 (1985): 21–35.

Bogue, M. B. *Fishing the Great Lakes: An Environmental History, 1783–1933.* Madison: University of Wisconsin Press, 2000.

Brinkmann, T. *Von der Gemeinde zur "Community": Jüdische Einwanderung in Chicago, 1840–1900.* Studien zur Historischen Migrationsforschung, 10. Osnabrück: Universitätsverlag Rasch, 2002.

Centers for Disease Control and Prevention. "Achievements in Public Health, 1900–1999: Control of Infectious Diseases." *MMWR Weekly* 48, no. 29 (1999): 621–29.

The Chicago Record Cook Book. Chicago: Chicago Record, 1896.

Cooke, M. C. *Social Etiquette; or, Manners and Customs of Polite Society: Containing Rules of Etiquette for All Occasions . . . Forming a Complete Guide to Self-Culture.* N.p.: N.p., 1896.

Croly, J. C. *Jennie June's American Cookery Book: Containing Upwards of Twelve Hundred Choice and Carefully Tested Receipts; Embracing All the Popular Dishes, and the Best Results of Modern Science*

. . . *Also, a Chapter for Invalids, for Infants, One on Jewish Cookery* . . . New York: American News, 1870.

Crumpacker, B. *The Old-Time Brand-Name Cookbook: Recipes, Illustrations, and Advice from the Early Kitchens of America's Most Trusted Food Makers.* New York: Smithmark, 1998.

Cutler, I. *The Jews of Chicago: From Shtetl to Suburb.* Urbana: University of Illinois Press, 1996.

Davidis, H. *Pickled Herring and Pumpkin Pie.* Madison, WI: Max Kade Institute, 2003.

Davidson, A. *The Oxford Companion to Food.* Oxford: Oxford University Press, 1999.

Dillon, D. nd. "Hull-House Experiments with the New England Kitchen and Develops Programs in Homemaking." http://tigger.uic.edu/htbin/cgiwrap/bin/urbanexp/main.cgi?file=new/show_doc_search.ptt&doc=10.

Diner, H. R. *Hungering for America: Italian, Irish, and Jewish Foodways in the Age of Migration.* Cambridge: Harvard University Press, 2001.

Dowling, J. W. "Old School Medicine and Homeopathy." *The North American Review,* 134, no. 307 (1882): 578–600.

Dye, M. *Home Economics at the University of Chicago, 1892–1956.* Chicago: Home Economics Alumni Association, University of Chicago, 1972.

Eliot, G. *Romola.* 3 vols. London: Smith, Elder, 1862–63.

Farmer, F. M. *The Boston Cooking-School Cook Book: A Facsimile of the Original Edition.* 1896. New York: Gramercy, 1997.

Faust, A. B. *The German Element in the United States with Special Reference to Its Political, Moral, Social, and Educational Influence.* Vols. 1 and 2. Boston: Houghton Mifflin, 1909.

FitzSimmons, E. *Teach Me: An Ethnography of Adolescent Learning.* Oxford: International Scholars Publications, 1999.

Frankenstein, I. R. *Irma: A Chicago Woman's Story, 1871–1966.* Ed. E. F. Steinberg. Iowa City: University of Iowa Press, 2004.

Gillette, F. L. *White House Cook Book: A Selection of Choice Recipes Original and Selected, during a Period of Forty Years' Practical Housekeeping.* Chicago: R. S. Peale, 1887.

Greenbaum, F. K. *The International Jewish Cook Book: 1600 Recipes according to the Jewish Dietary Laws with the Rules for Kashering; The Favorite Recipes of America, Austria, Germany, Russia, France, Poland, Roumania, Etc., Etc.* New York: Bloch, 1918.

Goodwin, L. S. *The Pure Food, Drink, and Drug Crusaders, 1879–1914.* Jefferson, NC: McFarland, 1999.

Grivetti, L. E., J. L. Corlett, B. M. Gordon, and C. T. Lockett. "Food in American History, Part 6—Beef (Part 1): Reconstruction and Growth Into the 20th Century (1865–1910)." In *Nutrition Today* 39, no. 1 (2004): 18–25.

Haber, B. *From Hardtack to Home Fries.* New York: Free Press, 2002.

Haberlandt, F. *Die Sojabohne: Ergebnisse der Studien und Versuche über die Anbauwürdigkeit dieser neu einzuführenden Culturpflanze.* Wien: C. Gerold's Sohn, 1878.

Heller, J. G. *Isaac M. Wise: His Life, Work and Thought.* New York: Union of American Hebrew Congregations, 1965.

Hense-Jensen, W., and E. Bruncken. *Wisconsins Deutsch-Amerikaner bis zum Schluss des 19.Jahrhunderts.* Vol. 1. Milwaukee, WI: Verlag der Deutschen Gesellschaft (Germania), 1902.

Holly, Don. "Ensuring Freshness, Roasting at Home." *Virtual Coffee!* (Winter 1998). www.virtualcoffee.com/nov/fresh.html.

Hoobler, D., and T. Hoobler. *The German American Family Album.* New York: Oxford University Press, 1996.

James, H., Jr. "Portrait of a Lady," part 1. *Atlantic Monthly* (November 1880): 585–91.

Johnson, S. W., "Adulteration of Food." Abstract. *Manufacturer and Builder* 12, no. 12 (1880): 282.

Joselit, J. W. "'A Set Table': Jewish Domestic Culture in the New World, 1880–1950." In *Getting Comfortable in New York: The American Jewish Home, 1880–1950,* ed. S. L. Braunstein and J. W. Joselit, 21–73. New York: Jewish Museum, 1990.

Kaufman Kohler, Mrs., trans. *Gates of Jewish Heritage.* Vol. 6. Baltimore, 1861. 2–22.

Kellogg, E. E. *Science in the Kitchen: A Scientific Treatise on Food Substances and Their Dietetic Properties, Together with a Practical Explanation of the Principles of Healthful Cookery, and a Large Number of Original, Palatable, and Wholesome Recipes.* Chicago: Modern Medicine, 1893.

Kellogg, J. H. *The New Method in Diabetes.* Battle Creek, MI: Battle Creek Modern Medicine, 1917.

Kirshenblatt-Gimblett, B. "Kitchen Judaism." In *Getting Comfortable in New York: The American Jewish Home, 1880–1950,* ed. S. L. Braunstein and J. W. Joselit, 75–105. New York: Jewish Museum, 1990.

Krasner-Khait, B. "The Impact of Refrigeration." *History Magazine* (February/March 2002). www.history-magazine.com/refrig. html.

Latcha, J. A. "Railroads versus Canals." *North American Review* 166, no. 495 (1898): 200–226.

Levenstein, H. A. "The New England Kitchen and the Origins of Modern American Eating Habits." *American Quarterly* 32, no. 4 (1980): 369–86.

———. *Revolution at the Table: The Transformation of the American Diet*. New York: Oxford University Press, 1988.

Levy, E. *Jewish Cookery Book*. Philadelphia: W. S. Turner, 1871.

Lincoln, Mrs. D. A. [Mary]. "Extracts from Cookery; or Art and Science versus Drudgery and Luck." In *The Congress of Women: Held in the Woman's Building, World's Columbian Exposition, Chicago, U. S. A., 1893*. ed., M. K. O. Eagle, 138–42. Chicago: Monarch, 1894.

———. *Mrs. Lincoln's Boston Cook Book: What to Do and What Not to Do in Cooking*. Boston: Roberts Brothers, 1884.

Max Kade Institute. "Kaffee- und Teegesellschaften [Coffee and Tea Parties]." Teacher Resource 2. http://csumc.wisc.edu/mki/Education/EDTeachRes2.htm.

———. "The Story of Immigration as Told through Cookbooks." Teacher Resource 1. http://csumc.wisc.edu/mki/Education/EDTeachRes1.htm.

McWilliams, C. *A Mask for Privilege: Anti-Semitism in America*. Boston: Little, Brown, 1948.

Mitchell, J. "Cookbooks as a Social and Historical Document: A Scottish Case Study." Abstract. *Food Service Technology* 1, no. 1 (2001): 13.

Moritz, C. F., Mrs., and A. Kahn. *The Twentieth Century Cook Book*. 5th ed. New York: G. W. Dillingham, 1897–98.

Muret, E., D. Sanders, and H. Baumann, eds. *Muret-Sanders Encyklopädisches englisch-deutsches und deutsch-englisches Wörterbuch (ein Parallelwerk zu Sachs-Villatte's französisch-deutschem und deutsch französischem Wörterbuch) mit Angabe der Aussprache nach dem phonetischen System der Methode Toussaint-Langenscheidt. Grosse Ausg*. Berlin-Schöneberg: Langenscheidtsche verlagsbuchhandlung, 1899.

Parker, E. H. *The Handbook for Mothers: A Guide in the Care of Young Children*. Toronto: Belfords, Clarke, 1880.

Parloa, M. "The New England Kitchen." *The Century* 43, no. 2 (1891): 315–17.

Pereira, J., "A Treatise on Food and Diet." *The North American Review* 34, no. 5 (1862): 733–40.

Quentin, K. *Reisebilder und Studien aus dem Norden der Vereinigten Staaten von Amerika.* Arnsberg: Druck und Verlag von H. F. Grote, 1851.

Reiling, J. "100 Years Ago, January 7, 1905." *JAMA* 293 (2005): 100.

Reynolds, A. R. "Dr. Neeley's Report of the City of Chicago for the years 1897 and 1898." In *Report of the Department of Health.* Chicago: Press of Cameron, Amberg, 1898.

Richards, E. H. "Count Rumford, and His Work for Humanity." In *Plain Words about Food: The Rumford Kitchen Leaflets,* ed. E. H. Richards, 19–27. Boston: Rockwell and Church, 1899.

———. "The Rumford Kitchen Exhibit at the World's Columbian Exposition, Chicago, 1893." In *The Report of the Massachusetts Board of World's Fair Managers, Boston.* N.p.: N.p., 1894. http://libraries.mit.edu/archives/exhibits/esr/esr-rumford.html.

Rippley, L. J. *The Immigrant Experience in Wisconsin.* Boston: Twayne, 1985.

Rorer, Mrs. S. T. *Made-Over Dishes.* 10th ed. Philadelphia: Arnold, 1898. www.gutenberg.org/etext/6978.

Rundell, M. E. K. *The Experienced American Housekeeper; or, Domestic Cookery Formed on Principles of Economy for the Use of Private Families.* Hartford: Silas Andrus and Judd, 1833.

Rury, J. L. "Vocationalism for Home and Work: Women's Education in the United States, 1880–1930." *History of Education Quarterly* 24, no. 1 (1984): 21–44.

Salisbury, J. H. *The Relation of Alimentation and Disease.* New York, J. H. Vail, 1888.

Shapiro, L. *Perfection Salad.* New York: Modern Library, 2001.

Soluri, J. "Accounting for Taste: Export Bananas, Mass Markets, and Panama Disease." *Environmental History* 7, no. 3 (2002): 386–410.

Theophano, J. *Eat My Words: Reading Women's Lives through the Cookbooks They Wrote.* New York: Palgrave Macmillan, 2002.

———. "Recipes for Reverie." *Penn Arts and Science* (Summer 1996). www.sas.upenn.edu/sasalum/newsltr/summer96/Theophano.html.

Thomas, Lately [pseud.]. *Delmonico's: A Century of Splendor.* Boston: Houghton Mifflin, 1967.

Thompson, Mrs. J. S. R. "Soja Beans." *Southern Farm* 5, no. 3 (1889): 141.

Thoreau, H. D. *Walden.* 1854. Ed. J. L. Shanley. Princeton: Princeton University Press, 1971.

Wisconsin Sea Grant. "Fish of the Great Lakes: Carp." *Great Lakes Online.* www.seagrant.wisc.edu/greatlakesfish/carp.html.

Wright, C. D. *Eighteenth Annual Report, 1903: Cost of Living and Retail Prices of Food.* Washington, D.C.: Government Printing Office, 1904.

Young, Enoch P. "Hampton Reminiscences: The Housewife of 65 Years Ago—Part XII." *Exeter News-Letter* (c. 1899). www.hampton.lib. nh.us/hampton/history/oral/reminiscences12.htm.

Zeitlin, R. H. *Germans in Wisconsin.* Revised and expanded ed. Madison: State Historical Society of Wisconsin, 2000.

Zobrowski, M., and E. Herzog. *Life Is with People.* New York: Schocken Books, 1967.

RECIPE INDEX

Anise cookies, 173. *See also* Anise
  cookies *in Subject Index*
Asparagus soup, 180. *See also*
  Asparagus soup *in Subject index*

Bacon, in veal breast with dressing,
  121
Bananas
  baked, 169. *See also* Bananas,
    baked *in Subject Index*
  blanc mange, 168. *See also*
    Bananas, blanc mange *in
    Subject Index*
  cream, 166. *See also* Bananas,
    banana cream *in Subject
    Index*
  pudding, steamed, 167. *See also*
    Bananas, pudding, steamed
    in Subject Index
Beauregard eggs, 146. *See also* Eggs,
  Beauregard *in Subject Index*
Beef
  chuck roast or pot roast, 129,
    132
  Hamburg steak, 176. *See also*
    Hamburg steak *in Subject
    Index*
  meat, deviled, 143. *See also*
    Meat, deviled *in Subject
    Index*
  in rice soup, 129

in vegetable soup, 132
Beverages
  coffee, 102. *See also* Coffee *in
    Subject Index*
  eggnog, 181. *See also* Eggnog *in
    Subject Index*
Blackberry cream, 162. *See also*
  Blackberry cream *in Subject
  Index*
Bread
  bread torte (*Brod Tort*), 103.
    *See also Brod Tort in Subject
    Index*
  day-old, in bread pudding, 104,
    105
  whole-wheat bread, excellent,
    117. *See also* Whole-wheat
    bread, excellent *in Subject
    Index*
Bread pudding No. 1 (*Brod
  Pudding*), 104. *See also Brod
  Pudding in Subject Index*
Bread pudding No. 2 (*Brod
  Pudding*), 105. *See also Brod
  Pudding in Subject Index*
Bread torte (*Brod Tort*), 103.
  *See also Brod Tort in Subject
  Index*
Breast of veal with dressing, 121. *See
  also* Breast of veal *in Subject
  Index*

Brown cookies, 174. *See also* Brown cookies (Friedman) *in Subject Index*

Button cookies, 172. *See also* Button cookies *in Subject Index*

Cake

    caramel cake, 110. *See also* Caramel cake *in Subject Index*

    chocolate cake, 111. *See also* Chocolate cake *in Subject Index*

    cream sponge, 108. *See also* Cream, sponge cake *in Subject Index*

    cup cake no. 1, 113. *See also* Cupcakes *in Subject Index*

    cup cake no. 2, 114. *See also* Cupcakes *in Subject Index*

    maple sugar cake, 109. *See also* Maple sugar cake *in Subject Index*

    sponge cake *(Spongue Cake)*, 107. *See also* Spongue cake *in Subject Index*

Caramel cake, 110. *See also* Caramel cake *in Subject Index*

Caramel icing, 110

Celery

    au jus, 127. *See also* Celery, au jus *in Subject Index*

    creamed, 125

    for garnish, 149. *See also* Celery, curled, for garnish *in Subject Index*

    oysters with, 142. *See also* Celery, oysters with *in Subject Index*

    salad, 150. *See also* Celery, salad *in Subject Index*

    stew, 126. *See also* Celery, stew in stock *in Subject Index*

Cherry salad, 151. *See also* Cherry salad *in Subject Index*

Chicken, broiled, 175. *See also* Chicken, broiled, for children *in Subject Index*

Chocolate

    blanc mange, 179. *See also* Chocolate, blanc mange *in Subject Index*

    in bread torte *(Brod Tort)*, 103

    in brown cookies, 174

    cake, 111. *See also* Chocolate, cake *in Subject Index*

    frosting, 112. *See also* Chocolate, frosting *in Subject Index*

Chuck roast or pot roast

    in rice soup, 129

    in vegetable soup, 132

Cider vinegar, in sour fish, 134

Coffee, 102. *See also* Coffee *in Subject Index*

Cookies

    anise, 173. *See also* Cookies, anise *in Subject Index*

    brown, 174. *See also* Cookies, brown *in Subject Index*

    button, 172. *See also* Cookies, button *in Subject Index*

Corn meal, in johnnycake *(Johnny Cake)*, 116

Cornstarch

    in mayonnaise *(Mayonnaissee)*, 152

    in sauce for fish, 137

Cream

    banana cream, 166. *See also* Bananas, banana cream *in Subject Index*

    blackberry cream, 162. *See also* Blackberry cream *in Subject Index*

    cakes (popovers), 171. *See also* Cream, cakes *in Subject Index*

    fresh, in sponge cakes, 22

    puffs, 170. *See also* Cream, puffs

Filling
    for cream cakes, 171
    for cream puffs, 170
    maple sugar filling, 109
Fish, 133. *See also* Fish *in Subject
    Index*
    baked, 138
    scalloped, 139
    sharp fish no. 1, 135
    sharp fish no. 2, 136
    sour fish, 134
Freekeh (dried green wheat) in
    green kern soup, 130
French potatoes, 119. *See also* French
    potatoes *in Subject Index*
Frosting
    caramel icing, 110
    chocolate frosting, 112
Fruits
    banana blanc mange, 168. *See
        also* Bananas, blanc mange
        in Subject Index
    banana cream, 166. *See also*
        Bananas, banana cream *in
        Subject Index*
    banana pudding, steamed, 167.
        See also Bananas, pudding,
        steamed *in Subject Index*
    bananas, baked, 169. *See also*
        Bananas, baked *in Subject
        Index*
    blackberry cream, 162. *See also*
        Blackberry cream *in Subject
        Index*
    cherry salad, 151. *See also*
        Cherry salad *in Subject
        Index*
    grape pie, 164. *See also* Grape
        pie *in Subject Index*
    prune pie, 165. *See also* Prune
        pie *in Subject Index*
    raspberry tart, 163. *See also*
        Raspberry tart, cream *in
        Subject Index*

Garnishes, celery for, 149. *See also*
    Celery: curled, for garnish *in
    Subject Index*
Grape pie, 164. *See also* Grape pie *in
    Subject Index*
Green kern soup, 130. *See also* Green
    kern soup *in Subject Index*
Green peas, 120. *See also* Green peas
    in Subject Index

Hamburg steak, 176. *See also*
    Hamburg steak *in Subject
    Index*
Hazelnuts, in cherry salad, 151

Jelly roll, 106. *See also* Jelly rolls *in
    Subject Index*
Johnnycake (*Johnny Cake*), 116. *See
    also* Johnny cake *in Subject
    Index*

Kisses, 158. *See also* Kisses *in Subject
    Index*

Lemons, in orange marmalade
    (*Orange Marmelade*), 118

Maize-based breads. *See* Johnny cake
    in Subject Index
Maple sugar cake, 109. *See also*
    Maple sugar cake *in Subject
    Index*
Maple sugar filling, 109. *See also*
    Maple sugar filling for cake *in
    Subject Index*
Mayonnaise (*Mayonnaissee*), 152.
    See also Mayonnaissee *in
    Subject Index*
Meat
    chicken, broiled, 175
    deviled, 143. *See also* Meat,
        deviled *in Subject Index*
    Hamburg steak, 176. *See also*
        Hamburg steak *in Subject*

Spanish cream, 178. *See also* Spanish cream *in Subject Index*

Spinach *(Spinnage)*, 128. *See also Spinnage* (spinach) *in Subject Index*

Split peas, in peas soup, 131. *See also* Peas soup *in Subject Index*

Sponge cake *(Spongue Cake)*, 107. *See also* Spongue cake *in Subject Index*

Stew, celery, 126. *See also* Celery, stew in stock *in Subject Index*

Surprise sausages, 144. *See also* Sausages, surprise *in Subject Index*

Sweet bread

    bread pudding No. 1 *(Brod Pudding)*, 104. *See also Brod pudding* (no. 1) *in Subject Index*

    bread pudding No. 2 *(Brod Pudding)*, 105. *See also Brod pudding* (no. 2) *in Subject Index*

    bread torte *(Brod Tort)*, 103. *See also Brod Tort in Subject Index*

    jelly roll, 106. *See also* Jelly roll *in Subject Index*

    johnnycake *(Johnny Cake)*, 116. *See also* Johnny cake *in Subject Index*

    muffins, 115. *See also* Muffins *in Subject Index*

Sweetbreads, baked, 123. *See also* Sweetbreads. baked *in Subject Index*

Tapioca, in grape pie, 164

Tomato

    sauce for fish, 138. *See also*

    Tomato, sauce for baked fish *in Subject Index*

    soup, 177. *See also* Tomato, soup *in Subject Index*

Veal breast, with dressing, 121. *See also* Veal, stuffed breast of *in Subject Index*

Vegetable dishes. *See also* Tomato

    asparagus soup, 180. *See also* Asparagus soup *in Subject Index*

    celery, creamed, 125

    celery au jus, 127. *See also* Celery, au jus *in Subject Index*

    celery salad, 150. *See also* Celery, salad *in Subject Index*

    celery stew, 126. *See also* Celery, stew in stock *in Subject Index*

    French potatoes, 119. *See also* French potatoes *in Subject Index*

    green peas, 120. *See also* Green peas *in Subject Index*

    spinach *(Spinnage)*, 128. *See also Spinnage* (spinach) *in Subject Index*

Vegetable soup, 132. *See also* Vegetable soup *in Subject Index*

Wheat, in green kern soup, 130

Wheat biscuits

    in oysters in baskets, 141

    in prune pie, 165

Whole-wheat bread, excellent, 117. *See also* Whole-wheat bread, excellent *in Subject Index*

Subject Index

Page numbers in italics refer to illustrations.

Cake: caramel cake, 24; chocolate, 25–26; cream, 68–69; cupcakes, 26–27, *97*; fancy cakes, 21; johnny cake, 28; maple sugar, 23; popover cream, 68–69; social interactions, role in, 18–19; sponge, 22–23; symbolism of, 19; traditional importance of, 18

Calves' foot broth, 79–80

Canned and tinned foods: economy of, 34; industry for, 35; Caramel cake, 24; Celeriac, 41

Celery: au jus, 39; availability of, 38; curled, for garnish, 54; nutritional properties of, 55, 188n13; oysters with, 46; recipes, 38–39; salad, 54; stew in stock, 39

Chemistry, application to cooking, 82–83

Chemistry of Cooking and Cleaning (Richards), 14

Cherry salad, 56

Chicago: Germans in, 5–7; meatpacking industry, 34; middle class, 6

Chicago Daily Tribune: "Bachelor Shows Them How To Cook" column, 49; fashionable events reporting, 189n17

Chicago Kitchen Garden Association, 194n40

Chicago Record, "Meals For A Day" recipe column, 28

The Chicago Record Cook Book (Chicago Record), 28, 55, 65

Chicken: broiled, for children, 76; cost of, 190n6

Children: lunch meals for, 76; "Pure Food for Pupils" program, 86

Chocolate: blanc mange, 79; cake, 25–26; frosting, 26; nutritional benefits of, 25

Cinnamon, oil of, 90

Cleanliness, 92–93; in kitchen and home, 87

Cleveland, Mrs. Grover, 61

Cleveland Baking Powder Company, 80

Coffee: as common beverage, 19; roasting and grinding beans for, 20

Coffee and tea parties, 19

Coffee House at Hull-House, 86

Color themes for meals, 59–60

Commercial food canning: history of, 35; prices of, 35

Consumptives, ivory jelly for, 90

Cookbooks: convalescents, recipes for, 75–76; expense of, 80; free, 191n12; nonkosher, 44–45

Cookery, art of, 18

Cookies, 69–70; anise, 70; brown (Friedman), 71; button, 70

"Cookies" (poem), 69–70

Cooking: as an appetizing process, 1; experimentation with, 91; importance of, 2; labor intensity of, 40; practicing, 13; supervision of, 92–93; thrift and economy in, 47–48

Corn, 27

Cream: banana, 68; blackberry, 65; cakes, 68–69; in fruit desserts, 64; puffs, 68–69; sauce, 37–38; sponge cake, 23

Creamed foods, 190n38

Croly, J., 22

Crumpacker, Betty, 191n10

Culinary innovations and inventions: Aladdin oven ("cooker"), 35–36, 86; baking powder, 21–22; effect on German traditions, 10–11; flat frying pans, 51

Cupcakes, 26; cup cake (no. 1), 27, *97*; cup cake (no. 2), 27

Custard: in fruit desserts, 64; orange, 62

Davis, Mary, 76
Desserts: banana blanc mange, 68; banana pudding, steamed, 68; bananas, baked, 68; blackberry cream, 65; cream cakes, 68–69; cream puffs, 68–69; custard, 62, 64; of fruits, 64; kisses, 62; raspberry tart, cream, 66. *See also* Pies
Deutsches Beefsteak auf Hamburg Art (Hamburg steak), 77
Diabetics: diets for, 88; nut flour bread for, 89
Dietary laws, keeping or not, 7–8, 185n8
Diet Kitchen at Hull-House, 84–86
Dinner: noontime, 10; traditional, 33
Dinner parties, 10; preparation for, 71
Diseases, 73–74
Domestic arts, education in, 12
Domestic science, founding of field, 14
Domestic science movement, 13–14; food chemistry data, 50; messages of, 91–92
Dowling, J. W., 88
Dr. Pierce's Common Sense Medical Advisor (Pierce), 190n1
Dutch ovens, 35–36
Dyspepsia, 188n21
Dyspeptics: diets for, 81–82, 87–88; graham flour for, 88; meals prepared for, 81; Salisbury steak for, 77

E. R. Durkee Company, 80
Edible flowers, 61
Eggnog, 79
Eggs: Beauregard, 52; dishes made with, 49–53; leftover, 50; omelets, 51; in salad dressings, 57; salad of, 52–53; stuffed, 52; yelk (yolk), 191n9
Eingedämpft Fleisch (Pot Roast), 36–37
Einhorn, David, 183n5
Eliot, George, 2, 184n3
The Experienced American Housekeeper; or, Domestic Cookery Formed on Principles of Economy for the Use of Private Families (Rundell), 12
Experts, recipes by, 80

Family favorites, 72
Fancy cakes, 21
Farmer, Fannie, 50
Faust, Albert Bernhardt, 6, 11
Felsenthal, Bernard, 183n4, 185n8
"First Cook Book": art of cookery philosophy in, 18; asides in, 34, 66; English and German language use, 18; menu plans, 33; newspaper and magazine recipes in, 23; selections, rationale behind, 3
Fish: availability and cost of, 41, 188n14; baked, 43–44; recipe, 42; scalloped, 44; sharp fish (no. 1), 42; sharp fish (no. 2), 43; sour fish, 42
Fleming, Harriet, 78
Flour: adulterations in, 30, 187n19; graham, 88; price of, 34; whole wheat, 30
Food and its preparation: aesthetic enhancements, 55; cost and accessibility, 34; hygienic techniques, 91–92; length of storage times, 34; as perspective on society's values, 10; preservation, 91–92
Forty-eighters (*Achtundvierzigers*), 6

Frankenstein, Irma (Rosenthal): cooking, appeal of, 15; cooking, experimenting with, 92–93; cooking, supervision for, 93; creamed foods, cooking, 190n38; health of, 73; Jewish community life participation, 183n4; parents' families' immigration, 8–9; poor, dispensing food to, 84

Frankenstein, Victor S., 1

French potatoes, 35, *94*

Fruit salad, 56

Fruits: availability of, 63–64; bananas, 67–68; blackberries, 65–66; in desserts, 64; fresh, 62–63; grapes, Concord, 66; raspberries, 66; transportation of, 63–64

Frying pans: flat, 51; "spiders," 51

Garnishes, 55; curled celery, 54

Gehacktes Rindfleischas (Hamburg steak), 77

Gelatine, 79–80, 191n10

Germ theory, 74–75

German beer gardens, 9

German communities: little Germany (*Kleindeutschland*) appearances of, 9; order (*ordnung*) of, 9

German immigrants: in Chicago, 5–7; diversity of language and culture among, 7; Gentiles and Jews, 7; immigration in family groups, 8–9; salads of, 53

German women: expectations of, 9; spheres of operation, 9; as teachers of next generation, 11; traditional meal preparation, 10; virtues of, 11

Gout sufferers, diets for, 89

Grape pie, 67

Grapes, Concord, 66

Green kern soup, 40, *94*

Green peas, 35, *94*

Greenbaum, Florence Kreisler, 3

Haberlandt, Friedrich, 88

Hamburg steak, 76–77

Harland, Marion, 28, 63

Hazelnuts, 56

Health benefits of foods, 55

Health food stores, 86–87

Health foods: articles on, 81–82; availability of, 87; palatability of, 90–91

Herzog, Elizabeth, 19

Home Economics: A Guide to Household Management (Parloa), 191n14

Homemaking versus housekeeping, 2

Hospitality toward visitors, 10, 19

Housekeeping versus homemaking, 2

Hull-House Kitchen, 84–85, 192n20

Hygiene: in kitchen, xiii, 13–14, 75, 84, 91–92; machine-kneaded versus hand-kneaded bread, 89; for meals for invalids, 83

Indian dumplings, 27

Indigestion, 188n21. *See also* Dyspeptics

Ingredients: handful and pinch methods, 28; versus seasonings, 91; unadulterated, 91; visually estimated, 24; volume measurements, 13, 26; weight measurements, 28–29, 70

Inter-Ocean daily recipes, 28

The International Jewish Cook Book: 1600 Recipes According to the Jewish Dietary Laws with the Rules for Kashering; The Favorite Recipes of America,

Michigan Seventh-Day Adventist
    sanitarium kitchen, 86
Modern conveniences: baking
    powder, 21–22; canned and
    tinned foods, 35; gas stoves
    and electricity, 11; packaged
    goods, 80
Moritz, Mrs. C. F., 14–15
Mrs. Lincoln's Boston Cook Book, 14
Muffins, 26–27
Murphy, John B., 90

Nason, Edith, 85
Nasturtium sandwiches, 61
Near West Side neighborhood, 5
*The New England Farmer: A Monthly
    Journal Devoted to Agriculture,
    Horticulture, and Their Kindred
    Arts and Sciences,* 190n34
New England Kitchen, 82–85,
    192n20
Newspaper and magazine recipes,
    14, 23. *See also recipes by name*
Nut flours, 89
Nutrition, health benefits of foods,
    55
Nuts: in bread, 82, 89; hazelnuts, 56

One-pot dishes, 35–36
Oranges: cost of, 189n24; in custard,
    62; in *marmelade* (marmalade),
    29–30
Organ meats for sick and
    convalescents, 37
Oysters, 44; availability and cost of,
    46, 188n18; in baskets, 45–46;
    with celery, 46; deviled, 45

Packaged goods: advertising for, 80;
    spending money on, 22
Pan gravy, 37
Parloa, Maria, 82, 191n14
Pastry dough, 64–65
Peanuts, availability of, 61

Peas, green, 35, *94*
Peas soup, 40–41
Pereira, Jonathan, 25
Physiological chemistry
    investigations, 50
Pie-crust, 64, *95*
Pies, 66–67; grape, 67; prune, 67
Pittsburgh Platform of 1885, 183n4,
    185n8
Poor persons, meals prepared for, 84
Popover cream cakes, 68–69
Pot Roast (*Eingedämpft Fleisch*),
    36–37
Potatoes: croquettes stuffed with
    sausage (*Kartoffelroketten mit
    wienerwürst gefüllt*), 49; French,
    35, *94;* price of, 34
Poverty, and cooking, 47–48
*Praktisches Kochbuch für die
    Deutschen in Amerika* (Practical
    Cookbook for Germans in
    America) (Davidis), 13
Product advertisements, 80
Proportions, recording, 24
Protein in the diet, 50
Prune pie, 67
Prunes, 66; cost of, 189n28
Puddings: banana, steamed, 68;
    chocolate blanc mange, 79;
    Spanish cream, 78

Quick-bread recipes, 26

Railroad transportation, 63–64
Raisins, availability and cost of, 61,
    189n22
Raspberry tart, cream, 66
Recipes: by experts, 80; frugality
    of, 56; in newspapers, 14, 23;
    "scratch," 100; for sick persons,
    74–78; standardization of, 13;
    updating of Irma's, 100–101
Reform Judaism, 7–8, 183nn4–5,
    185n8

Theophano, Janet, 13, 80
Thomas, A. C., 53
Time-savers: canned and tinned foods, 35; one-pot dishes, 35–36
Tomato: sauce for baked fish, 44; soup, 78
Tuberculosis: malnutrition and, 190n1; oil of cinnamon for, 90
Twentieth Century Cook Book (Moritz and Kahn), 14–15
Twenty Years at Hull-House (Addams), 85
Typhoid fever, 77–78; asparagus soup for, 191n11

University of Chicago, courses in sanitary science, 194n40

Veal, stuffed breast of, 36
Vegetable soup, 41
Vegetables: seasonal availability, 38; washing, 1
Vegetarianism, 87, 192n24
Visitors, hospitality toward, 10, 19
Visually estimated ingredient amounts, 24
Vollkornbrot (whole-grain bread), 29
Volume measurements, 13, 26

Weight measurements, 28–29, 70
West Side Settlement House, 84
Wheat: dried and roasted, 40; shredded wheat biscuits, 45, 66–67
White sauce, 37
Whole-grain bread (*Vollkornbrot*), 5
Whole-wheat bread, excellent, 29
Whole-wheat flour: cost factors of, 30; nutritional value of, 187n18
Wine, in bread tortes, 20
Women: care and feeding of sick, 4, 75–76; domestic knowledge of, 12, 14, 92; household duties, 36; spheres of operation, 9; treasured recipes of, 5; working, 36. *See also* German women
Women's magazines: proliferation of, 75, 80; recipes in, 2, 4, 14, 23, 25

Yeast, 22, 29, 31; bread, 89; dyspeptics and, 81, 88
Yeast powder, 21–22
Yelk (yolk), 191n9
Young, Enoch P., 11

Zobrowski, Mark, 19